THE PRISONER PRESS PRESENTS

THE NATIONAL PRO BONO ATTORNEY DIRECTORY

JAILHOUSE LAWYER EDITION
2026

SAM FERRARO

National Pro Bono Attorney Directory
Jailhouse Lawyer Edition 2026
Copyright © 2024 by Sam Ferraro

THE PRISONER PRESS
P.O. Box 6053
100 South Belcher Road,
Clearwater, FL 33758
Website: theprisonerpress.com
Send comments, reviews, and all other inquiries to info@theprisonerpress.com

ISBN (paperback): 979-8-218-75824-0
ISBN (eBook): 979-8-218-75825-7

Printed in the United States of America
First printing: 2025 by the Prisoner Press, LLC

Cover design by 100covers.com

MISSION STATEMENT
It is the mission of The Prisoner Press to provide a multimedia platform to help prisoners and ex-offenders by giving them the information and resources they may need to make their time while incarcerated as productive and meaningful as possible as well as achieve success once they are paroled and released back into their community.

LIMIT OF LIABILITY/DISCLAIMER
The author and the publisher have made every attempt to provide the readers with accurate, up-to-date, and useful information. However, given the rapid changes taking place in today's world, some of the information in this book will inevitably change. Any addresses, phone numbers, or company and individual's information printed in this book are offered as a resource and are not intended in any way to be or imply an endorsement by the author or the publisher, nor does the author vouch for the existence, content, or services of these addresses, phone numbers, companies, or individuals beyond the life of this book. THEREFORE, the publisher shall not be liable for any losses or damages incurred in the progress of using the information within this book.

TABLE OF CONTENTS

■ ■ ■

Dedication

To My Amazing Parents:

Despite all the shit I've put you through – it's been an epic proportion of shit – you've never given up on me, even after everyone else in my life did. This book is proof of your support. Without you, none of what I've been able to accomplish would ever have been possible. There isn't enough money in the world to repay you for everything you've done for me. But, maybe, knowing I've finally found success in my life and have a promising future ahead of me is a good start.

Thank you, Mom and Dad

I love you both so much.

DEAR READER,

First off, I would like to begin by thanking you for buying my book and for supporting not only me but everyone at The Prisoner Press. It means the world to all of us who have worked so hard to bring you this Pro Bono Attorney Resource Directory, because without you, then there would be none of this. It's because of you all of this is even possible.

I sincerely hope that this book helps you in your quest to finding free and affordable legal representation, as it has for so many others across the country. As you can imagine, because I'm an incarcerated author, usually everything I try to do is an uphill battle and met with extreme challenges and difficulty. That especially includes promoting and trying to get the word out about my books to people on the outside and inmates in other prisons and county jails. That's why to help with this, if you found my book to be helpful, please go online, leave a review on Amazon, post about it on your social media, and spread the word about my book to family, friends, co-workers, and anyone you know that's incarcerated.

This is the very first book that I've published and is the first in my series, "The Sh*t Prisoners Need to Know." The Prisoner Press isn't just your average publishing company, and I'm definitely not your average author. So therefore, to understand my credibility and my perspective, experience, and knowledge, you first have to understand a little about me and the type of life that I've lived, which has taught me everything that I know and now share through my books. Because of the predominantly criminal and addict lifestyle I chose to live, I have spent most of my 20s and now the beginning of my 30s locked up, whether it was in county jail, state prison, or a court-ordered inpatient drug treatment rehab.

Most people if they were in my situation, 31 years old, with almost a decade already spent behind bars and now back again in prison for six more years, wasting the better parts of their 30s, they would've given up; most of them, well before even catching the new case and being sentenced to prison for the fourth time. I see it literally every day in prison. They give up on life, then break down and accept the fact they believe they're fated to an inevitable state of living between two equally as terrible life sentences: one out on the streets living as nothing more than a criminal and drug addict, and the other locked away in prison living a nonexistent life as an inmate, a fate that I had come way too close to falling into myself and undoubtedly would have if it hadn't been for the success I have had with my new-found legitimate hustle as an author and business owner, along with everything else I have been able to accomplish against all odds while incarcerated.

Then there are those like me who are different. We're the type who are too damn stubborn to ever give up and let the universe win or succumb to any ill-fated destiny that we didn't choose for ourselves. And although as beneficial as having such a strong, unyielding, and relentless personality can be, it just as easily can be the cause to your downfall, just as it has been mine countless times. It's caused so much destruction all throughout my life and has been the underlying reason that I've spent so many years of my life locked up. After I finish serving this six-year sentence, I will have all together a total of 14 years being locked up between county and state prison. Bruh, that's fucking crazy just thinking about it, especially given that I'll only be 36 years old when I get out. This is absolutely my last time. This is no longer the life I'm down with having now that I have proven to myself I can be so much more!

However, through all the setbacks, hard times, losses I've endured, and my best years wasted in prison, do you think that I've ever given up or lost my drive and ambition to become successful?

What do you think? FUCK, NO! Not even a little bit. I've just had to work that much harder and get it in different ways being that I'm limited to what all I can do because I'm incarcerated. But that has never stopped me. You're holding the proof in your hands right now of just how different I really am. Who goes to prison and through all of the adversity finds success and turns their sentence into a legitimate business venture and themselves into a published author and business owner? Me, that's who! And I've only just begun chasing all this legitimate money in the publishing game.

Very few people have sympathy for America's incarcerated population. And I get it. Growing up, I was taught not to either, even though deep down I never actually felt that way. I grew up watching COPS, as so many kids did in the early 2000's, and always found myself rooting for the bad guy rather than the police. But as I've gotten older, I've come to realize things are rarely so black and white. As human beings, we are inherently flawed, and there is never a good answer when it comes to imposing justice. Justice requires accountability on the part of the wrongdoer — and, in today's world, that accountability is usually dispensed in the form of fines, probation, community service, or incarceration. The intention seems to be ensuring that karma is being maintained — what goes around comes around, right?

Yeah, that's all well and good. And, sure, I agree with the basic principle of karma underlying justice.

Yet, there's something I do have a problem with.

Our judicial system is quick to dispense punishment whenever a normal citizen breaks one of their laws. And if they are unable to afford to hire adequate legal assistance, then they unfortunately open themselves up to potentially being taken advantage of by the very governing system that's in place to uphold justice in our society. Hell, they'll click those cuffs on you, lock you up, send you to jail, and weigh you down with exorbitant fines so fast and without a second thought. Then they'll nod approvingly and say "Justice has been served." To them, they're just upholding the balance of karma in the universe.

But what happens when it is an influential member of society who has the means to get the very best of legal representation? What happens when one of them gets caught doing something wrong? Does the system pursue justice with the same zeal they display when they're seeking to punish a regular Joe like you and me? Because in a democratic society, we invest great power in our government, and in return, we expect the government we've empowered to use their sense of discretion and act fairly when exercising the powers we've given them.

Unfortunately, however, that doesn't always happen.

I have been through the court system more times than I care to admit, and I know all too well how it is when you have your own hired attorney and when you do not. I only wished that there was a book like this when I was going through my legal battles with a public defender. It would have changed everything if I would have had a pro bono attorney representing me. That is why I wanted to write this book. And it will be the first book in my series, because nothing like this — that my team and I have been able to find — even exists to help people like you and me who can't afford to have the best attorneys representing us, but at the same time, don't want to be screwed by the system because of it.

This book is one that honestly I hope you never actually need, but in the unfortunate case you find yourself in a situation that you do, it's here to help you. And if you do use it to find a free or affordable attorney to represent you in your criminal case, I hope that it will be the last time you ever need to pick this book up again if you're in the criminal lifestyle, struggling with addiction, or incarcerated and you want a better life for yourself but don't know where to begin.

The next two books of my series, "The Jailhouse Financial Playbook" and "How To Beat Parole At Their Own Game," are an absolute must have! They will provide you with the game plans, step-by-step guides, resources, and everything else you'll need to learn how to hustle legally, obtain financial independence and success while incarcerated, overcome addiction, get out and stay out of jail, beat parole, unlock the best version of yourself, and change your life forever!

I'm going to let you in on something that you probably won't believe. It's that no matter who you are, how much money you have, or where you are, whether you're incarcerated or out on the streets, you can just as easily find a good lawyer. And unlike the rich and influential who pay top dollar for their legal counsel, you'll have the same level of representation that they do, only you won't pay anything for it. And I'm going to help you do it. Throughout my book, I give you all the resources and cheat codes that you'll need to find and obtain the best possible attorney FOR FREE.

Just as it is with everything challenging, whether it be quitting drugs and staying sober, starting a business, getting a college degree, or whatever it is you're trying to do, the only thing that can stop you from being successful is you. We're always going to be our own worst enemy and find excuses for everything. Believe me, I know all about that. Only now, with this book, I have eliminated all the excuses you could come up with as to why you can't find a lawyer to represent you. So now you can use all your energy on actually doing it rather than trying to find reasons why you can't.

YOU CAN'T BECAUSE YOU'RE LOCKED UP...

Bruh. That's like the easiest excuse ever that you can use for just about anything. And it's also the most absolutely untrue and bullshit excuse! After reading this book, you won't ever be able to legitimately use that excuse again. That's because you'll have all the information and resources you need to successfully find a pro bono attorney. Being locked up isn't the permanent roadblock preventing you from doing what you want that many think it is.

It's just another obstacle in your path to freedom and success that you'll have to figure out how to get around just as I had to when I had to figure out how to overcome all the restrictions and limitations of being incarcerated to publish a book and start my own company. And after hard work and dedication, I overcame all the challenges and prevailed. Everything that I have done legitimately thus far and every dollar I've made has been from inside prison.

So if that's what is stopping you, then you discovered the right series, because everything in my books are predominantly for prisoners and ex-offenders.

YOU CAN'T BECAUSE YOU DON'T KNOW ANYTHING ABOUT PRO BONO ATTORNEYS OR WHERE TO FIND ONE...

My first time going through the court system as a criminal defendant, I was 18 years old, and I didn't know shit about the law, the judicial process, my rights, or anything. The only thing that I knew back then was how to fuck my life up and getting into trouble, but getting out of it was an entirely different story. I knew nothing about defending myself, hiring a lawyer, or that there was even such a thing as a pro bono lawyer. As a consequence of that, I only ever had court-appointed public defenders representing me for most of all my criminal cases, and as a result of that, I have the corresponding convictions and years spent in prison to show just how ineffective court-appointed lawyers can be.

Then in 2021, thirteen years after my first court appearance, seven criminal cases and seven public defenders and seven convictions later, I hired my first ever paid attorney to represent me on a drug case that I had caught in the midst of the pandemic. That was the very first case out of all the cases I've had throughout my life that I actually didn't get convicted of, all because I had hired an attorney. It wasn't until a year later in 2022 when I caught the case that I'm serving time for currently that I learned that it was actually possible to find a real attorney that will represent you for no costs.

It was an extremely difficult process finding a pro bono attorney from county jail, but ultimately, I was able to find one and get him to represent me for free. Let's put it this way: I was facing over a dozen charges, many of them serious felonies, including grand theft auto, assault with a deadly weapon, and aggravated assault with bodily injuries on a police officer, and my first plea deal from the district attorney was 20 to 40 years. And without any question with a public defender, I'd be serving that 20 years right now. However, with the pro bono attorney I found to represent me, he managed to get me a three-to-six year deal that no one believed was even possible, most of all not me. That's the power of knowledge. If it wasn't for me learning about pro bono lawyers, doing the research and putting in the leg work to find one, my life would be a whole lot worse off, as I'd likely be doing a minimum of 20 years in prison.

That reason, among many others, was what sparked my dedication to learn as much as I could about finding and obtaining a pro bono attorney and write this book for all who have the need for an attorney but cannot afford one and don't know how to find free legal representation.

Fortunately for you, most of the leg work has already been done for you. You have in your hand something I would've killed for in my earlier life going through all my legal battles. This is your cheat code. With this resource, you will have everything that you will need to find a pro bono attorney.

YOU THINK THAT JUST BECAUSE I WAS ABLE TO FIND AN ATTORNEY FOR FREE DOESN'T MEAN THAT YOU WILL HAVE THE SAME SUCCESS...

That's exactly the self-defeating mentality that will prevent you from ever accomplishing anything worthwhile in your life, just as it did for so many years with me. And it's that kind of negative bullshit thinking you're going to have to change and do it quickly if you're ever going to even have any shot at becoming wealthy and successful, let alone finding a pro bono attorney. Stop trying to compare yourself with others. That never ends well, and it'll only drive you crazy. Trust me here. It has absolutely nothing to do with whether or not you're like me or getting lucky, because, straight up, there is nothing that I have done that you can't do yourself as long as you put the work in and follow my game plan.

YOU CAN'T GET GOOD LEGAL REPRESENTATION BECAUSE YOU ARE BROKE AND DON'T THINK YOU HAVE ENOUGH MONEY TO HIRE AN ATTORNEY...

Bruh, you really think you're the only one in that situation, because you're not. Just about everyone who's locked up or who has just come home on parole doesn't have any money, especially enough to afford the expensive costs of hiring a lawyer. That's one of the biggest challenges that so many face. Inmates fighting their new charges from the county jail who don't want to get railroaded need an attorney to represent them, but because they can't afford it, their only option is a public defender, where they're only hope is to get a plea deal that doesn't completely screw them. And state prisoners who are in need of post-conviction assistance but don't have the money to afford it are stuck sitting in prison without any hope of getting help.

The truth is, affording legal assistance isn't only a challenge for inmates. Most normal, working-class people out there don't have the money either. Here's some crazy-sounding but true advice you should hold on to: Having money makes everything in life much easier, but here's the crazy thing. It's not actually necessary to have, because it's been my experience over and over again that as long as you want something bad enough, you'll find a way to get it. A perfect example of that is me.

I published this book and started my company my first year in prison when I was completely tapped out from blowing all of what little money I had on drugs and commissary in the county. Within my first couple months of coming upstate, I had run through the rest of my money and was broke as hell surviving off of nothing but my little $45 per month institutional work pay. I knew that I couldn't go through my entire bid being broke like that, and so I started coming up with different creative ways to hustle and make enough money to afford to hire a company out in California to help me self-publish my book. So, yeah. You can't get much lower than where I had started from.

In fact, if it wasn't for me having to go through that struggle in the beginning of my bid, I never would've developed the money-hungry desperation that had pushed me to think outside the box and come up with new ways — above and beyond the typical played-out jailhouse hustles — to earn money from the other inmates on my block and all over the prison. That determination was what got me off the bunk, out of my self-defeating feelings, and how I came to create my game plan. That game plan, the same one I break down for you to follow in my second book, mapped out exactly how I would become wealthy and successful, not just while I was incarcerated, but for the rest of my life.

Without that struggle, without that desperation and money-motivated drive, I never would've picked up a pen to create the game plan, write this book, or ever come up with the idea to start my own publishing company. And, of course, without the incredible success of both my book series and my company, "The Prisoner Press," I never would've accomplished any of the many other things that I've been able to do over the past years and be where I am today, which is still in prison, but unlike how I had come in. Now having worked so hard and pushed through so many barriers in and out of prison, I'm on an entirely different level of the game.

I owe everything to the struggle that I have endured, because as hard as the journey has been, it not only has made me into the successful author and legit, paper-chasing entrepreneur that I am today, it has taught me so many valuable lessons. I have learned so much about so many different things: money, business, life, people, the law, and most importantly myself and what all I'm really capable of accomplishing even while at my lowest.

Over the past years, I have become an expert on many different subjects, including the many different ways anyone, regardless of their background, financial situation, or whether they're in prison or out on the streets, can make all kinds of money hustling legitimately. But one of the things I have learned and probably the most important of all is that today being a criminal just ain't the wave anymore. And more than that, crime, the entire fast lifestyle and everything that comes along with it, is played out.

This isn't me selling out or switching up all of sudden because now I've gone legit, got a little bit of money under me, or whatever. That's never the time I'll be on. I'm always going to be me. I'm not saying this to try and appeal to what society deems acceptable or to be politically correct. That is not my argument here, nor is it ever my intention to do so. No. I'm saying this to be real with you and try to hopefully get through to you to save your life. Even though if you're anything like the younger me, then you're probably too stubborn to listen to anything that anyone has to say and only learn from the hardest ways possible. But, then again, the younger me never would've picked this book up despite needing it, so maybe there's a chance...

I will be the first to admit that back not that long ago when I was out there living the fast lifestyle, no one could have ever convinced me to stop living the way that I was and walk away from any of it. There was nothing that anyone could have told me, because I knew the risks I was taking and the consequences that came with them. And as crazy as it may sound to all those reading this who never lived that type of life and so familiar with those who have, I was perfectly okay with it. To me, what would become my ultimate demise at the time had felt like my best life I was living, and you couldn't tell me otherwise.

It took me doing something incredibly stupid and dangerous, getting caught, convicted, and sent to prison for a fourth time for me to finally have enough and want something more out of life than just fast money, easy girls, and drugs. Taking that long bus ride upstate, something inside me just clicked. That's when I knew I was done risking my freedom, and more importantly, my life out there because I wanted to run the streets and live the fast life just to end up inevitably losing everything that I worked to gain and back in prison.

Admittedly I was more addicted to that crazy ass, high octane, fast money, drug fueled, can't-tell-me-shit lifestyle and how I really lived every day out there like I was the Prince of, fucking, Philly, than I was to anything else, including even getting high, which was a close second. As with any bad addiction, living the fast criminal lifestyle, there was never any middle ground. Either you were all the way up, living what felt like your absolute best life, or you weren't, and you were all fucked up drowning at your rock bottom. But the really scary thing about addiction is, as horrible as the low's always are, it's the times that you're up feeling the full effects of the high that hooks you and makes you chase after it no matter what the costs. And once you're addicted, once whatever it is has its hooks deep in you, whether it's drugs, sex, or living the fast lifestyle like it was for me, the highs are so strong and euphoric that you make yourself believe that it's worth enduring the even stronger lows and doing whatever you have to just to get back up to that level of feeling like you're King of the Universe, or in my case, Prince of Philly.

When I was up, I had more money than I did sense, as I'm sure many reading this can relate with, and because of that, my dumbass wasted every bit of money that I made on all the wrong shit: an entourage of fake friends who only were around for the good time and to use me for whatever they could, expensive cars - and I'm not talking about buying them out right in cash. No. That would at least make some sense. I'm talking about renting them out every day for hundreds of dollars - renting out condos and million-dollar houses through Airbnb, buying jewelry, designer clothing and sneakers, the best looking women money can buy - whether they were college girls, escorts, or porn stars - drugs - so much drugs, traveling in private jets, partying in every city, and any other stupid, meaningless thing I could think of wasting all my money on without ever once thinking about saving or investing any of it because I was young, dumb, and thought that was what living the good life was all about. Only if I had the sense to save and invest even just a fraction of the exorbitant amount of money I was bringing in back then, I would've been a millionaire ten times over by now, and there's no telling where I'd be right now - not in a prison cell; that's for certain!

As an addict, we're just one bad decision away from relapsing, fucking our lives up, and spiraling right back down to rock bottom, regardless how far we may have come. Scary thought, but it's the reality that we have to live with every day. And if I'm keeping it all the way real with all of you, even with my success and all the legitimate money that I'm making now, I would give it all up without a second thought if there was even the slightest possibility that I could go back to getting high and living my old criminal lifestyle as the Prince of Philly and get away with doing it without ending up back in prison or dead. But the way things are today out there on the streets, no matter what you may want to believe, those are really the only two outcomes.

Long gone are the days where you could actually have a real shot at having a successful long run in this life. And if you disagree, you're just lying to yourself because you're not yet ready to give up living the life. Because the reality is, nowadays it's just about impossible to hustle doing whatever you do, stack your money, invest it into something legitimate, and then get out of the game clean. Straight up, that shit is over. You're either going to fall victim of being outed by a confidential informant or caught by the police and sent to prison, and that's if you're lucky, because if not, you're going to end up getting taken out by some wild young boy or one of your op's and put on a t-shirt.

These young boys have turned the streets into a war zone so much so that you can't even hustle and make money out there anymore. Every day it seems like you're hearing about a shooting where someone got killed right out in public, because the streets have no mercy, and these kids have no regard for human life. To them, it's just like playing a first-person shooter video game. So that's why I say crime and that whole lifestyle is played all the way out. It's not strategically intelligent to do anymore, especially under today's circumstances. Not only are all the risks you have to take to commit a crime larger than they have ever been before, and the losses you'll end up taking will almost always outweigh whatever you've gained, but because with all of the legitimate opportunities out there that's available to everyone with today's technology and resources, it's not even necessary to do anymore.

For all those reasons and more, I don't know about you, but I'm through with the whole lifestyle of being a career criminal and drug addict. I refuse to once again be another statistic for recidivism ever again. It has become my passion to learn how to make more money legally than I ever did illegally, so that when I'm finally released from prison in the beginning of 2028 (or possibly even sooner if I'm granted parole), I can ball just as hard as I did when I was the Prince of Philly, except only this time I'll do it much smarter and without the risk of doing anything that would potentially ever send me back to prison or get me killed over.

Not only has it become my passion to learn it and create my own game plans from it to make money by hustling legally, but also to share that knowledge and teach it to others just like me who want to make just as much money and live the same lavish balling lifestyle as they did before when they were living the criminal lifestyle but do it now legitimately without any of the risks or dangers that come with it. That's exactly what this series – "The Sh*t Prisoners Need To Know" - is all about, starting with the National Pro Bono Attorney Resource Directory, the most important book every inmate and individual facing upcoming legal battles needs to have to help them find free or affordable legal representation.

Sincerely, Your Friend,

Sam Ferraro

INTRODUCTION

INTRODUCTION

Far too often in our lives, we want things to be easy, and when they aren't, our natural inclination is to place the blame somewhere else. We blame society, other people, our upbringing, genetics, or on some unforeseen circumstance – it doesn't matter, as long as we can avoid feeling responsible for not succeeding or living up to our own expectations. As a way to preserve our ego, we retreat into a default mindset of helplessness, rejecting the very notion that we have the power to change the daily reality of our lives and shape what the future will be like. In fact, many of us get to a point in life where, mentally, we end up just giving up. We in turn make ourselves believe cop-outs such as, "well, this is just the way my life is, and I'm not smart enough, rich enough, or attractive enough to do anything about it, so, screw it." If we buy into this thinking, we eventually begin to believe that we aren't really responsible for the state of our existence, that every circumstance of our life is determined by forces outside of our control and that we might as well accept failure and lower our expectations for ourselves and our future.

My friends, do not buy into this self-defeatist narrative. If you do, you might as well close this book and pass it on to someone who can use it. Your mindset determines how much determination and effort you will put into the success of your life. Finding an attorney to take your case on pro bono will not be an easy task. Unwilling to put the necessary work in, you will not likely succeed. However, if you are, then this book will be a vital tool for you. No matter how fucked up you may be right now and no matter how insurmountable the obstacles in your life might seem, nothing is ever impossible!

All right. You might be in trouble with the law or incarcerated. Sure, you might've made some really poor decisions in life. And, yeah, society may have labeled you as a lost cause who's incapable of turning things around. Well, I'm here to tell you that society is full of shit. You can change. You can make a comeback and fix your life. You can overcome whatever troubling circumstances you may be facing and achieve every dream you have that might have once seemed unattainable. Don't get it fucked up. Nothing worth doing is ever easy. It's going to take work. It's going to take discipline. And it's going to require you to have some really honest and uncomfortable conversations with yourself. However, if you're willing to set aside your pride and truly get serious about achieving your goals, whether it's becoming a millionaire or finding a pro bono attorney, it can be done. The limits of your potential are defined only by the extent to which you're willing to work towards your dreams.

My life is proof of that.

Let's get started.

CHAPTER 1

1. WHAT A PRO BONO ATTORNEY IS AND WHERE TO FIND ONE

Secrets to Finding a Pro Bono Attorney

Lawyers are expensive. You know that already. In fact, the financial costs of having good legal representation are often so high that the average person can't even afford an attorney. But what does that mean for the average guy in prison? Are we screwed? Does that mean "justice" is available only to the wealthiest members of society? Unfortunately, it often seems like it, but it isn't supposed to be that way. After all, according to the U. S. Judicial System, access to legal counsel is a basic human right -- and a founding principle when it comes to fairness before the law. Yet, far too often, the rights of the common man get trampled beneath the feet of those with deeper pockets simply because your average Joe doesn't have the financial resources to afford adequate legal representation.

That's why pro-bono lawyers play a crucial role. By offering their legal services free of charge, some attorneys give the poor a pinprick of light at the end of the tunnel.

The Difference Between Pro-Bono and Legal Aid

"Pro-Bono" is a Latin phrase translating to "for the public good." And, in the legal process, the phrase pertains to work a lawyer does at no cost to their client. Similarly, a "legal aid" office is a group of lawyers who represent clients that can't afford to pay for legal services. The difference is this: Legal Aid groups are generally composed of full-time professionals who deal exclusively with the poor; whereas pro-bono attorneys work mostly with fee-paying clients but will occasionally take on a case for free.

A common mistake amongst people seeking counsel free of cost is to assume that a pro-bono attorney is preferable than counsel offered by legal aid groups. While this might sometimes be true, it's more often the case that legal aid groups are more well-versed in the areas of the law that poor people most commonly seek assistance with (i.e., matters pertaining to welfare, housing, and consumer law.) So don't presume that if a non-legal aid attorney takes your case for free you're assured of a better outcome. Legal Aid groups are usually more experienced at handling the cases of poor and incarcerated clients.

That being said, most legal aid organizations tend to only take on civil cases, not criminal. This is because criminal defendants who can't pay for an attorney get court-appointed counsel (a public defender). So if you're looking to appeal a current criminal case, a better option would be to seek a pro-bono attorney, especially if you have a good legal issues. Because, while legal aid groups are often looking to effect broad legal reform, pro-bono attorneys tend to look for winnable individual cases that might polish their reputation. For instance, a hotshot criminal defense attorney might take on your case to show off what a great lawyer he is to potential paying clients (while also getting to look like "a man of the people").

Of course, though we all would like pro-bono attorneys to be a dime a dozen, the reality is that they aren't. States don't require pro-bono work as essential to maintaining a law license. But the American Bar Association does encourage all attorneys to dedicate at least 50 hours a year to volunteer legal counsel for those who otherwise couldn't afford representation.

Tips On Where to Start Your Pro-Bono Search

If you feel you need pro-bono counsel, see if you can have a loved one on the street look into your local or state bar association. If they visit the association's website, they may come across attorneys willing to take on select cases for free. Or they could always reach out to the state bar association directly.

Another option is to scout around a local law school or its website. Some law schools allow students under the supervision of qualified attorneys to take cases free of charge.

6.1 Voluntary Pro Bono Public Service

"Every lawyer has a professional responsibility to provide legal services to those unable to pay. In fulfilling this responsibility, the lawyer should provide legal services without fee or expectation of fee to:

"1) persons of limited means; or
"(2) charitable, religious, civic, community, governmental and educational organizations in matters that are designed primarily to address the needs of persons of limited means; and
"(3) individuals, groups or organizations seeking to secure or protect civil rights, civil liberties or public rights, or charitable, religious, civic, community, governmental and educational organizations in matters in furtherance of their organizational purposes, where the payment of standard legal fees would significantly deplete the organization's economic resources or would be otherwise inappropriate; or
"(4) activities for improving the law, the legal system or the legal profession."

"In addition, a lawyer voluntarily should contribute financial support to organizations that provide legal services to persons of limited means."

CHAPTER 2

2. PRO BONO ATTORNEY AND LEGAL AID STATE DIRECTORY

I have organized all the resources that my team and I have worked so hard to gather for you by individual state rather than by category of services offered. This directory is only a comprehensive list of attorneys, organizations, programs, and services for legal assistance. Although I have included some basic details for most of the listings, it is up to you to contact specific services and request more information. Almost every listing has an address for you to write to. For the few which do not and only have either a phone number or website, have your family contact them directly.

As this is the Prisoner Edition, I have included all the many resources geared specifically to incarcerated individuals. This directory has very few listings of defense attorneys, as there are just too many to list, and most do not advertise they take on pro bono cases. The attorneys that I do list mainly offer post-conviction services.

What are post-conviction services? If you have already been convicted of a crime and are currently incarcerated, there may still be legal help available to you. Post-conviction legal services help with primarily parole and appeals.

If you are found guilty of a crime, you have the constitutional right to file an appeal. And unless you are a jailhouse lawyer or well versed in law, and more than likely you're not, you will need an attorney to assist you through the legal process. There are time restrictions to file an appeal. Because of that, it is in your best interests to seek legal assistance as soon as you can after conviction.

If there had been an error made, regardless of how minimal it may be during the course of your trial, then you may have a good case to file an appeal. If you are successful with your appeal, then your conviction may be overturned, and you will be granted a new trial or, even better, be released and let go free. For a comprehensive list of appellate reasons, I have included all of the most common ones in Chapter 6.

ALABAMA

ACLU of Alabama
207 Montgomery Street, Ste. 910
Montgomery, AL 36104
(Phone) 334-262-0304
Email: info@aclualabama.org
Website: www.aclualabama.org

Aid to Inmate Mothers
Attn: Carol Potok
P. O. Box 986
Montgomery, AL 36101
(Phone) 334-262-2243
Email: carol@inmatemoms.org
Website: www.inmatemoms.org
Transitional program for mothers who are between 18 and 24 months of their release dates. Offer educational programs for women prisoners, release plans, and follow-up casework for one year after release. Arrange monthly visitation for mothers who do not already have transportation for their children. Provide outreach to children while their mothers are incarcerated.

Alabama CURE
P. O. Box 190504
Birmingham, AL 35219
(Phone) 205-481-3781

Alabama Equal Justice Initiative
Attn: Bryan Stevenson
114 North Hull Street
Montgomery, AL 36104-3796
(Phone) 334-269-1803

Alabama Legal Help
Alabama Legal Help. org
Legal Services Alabama
(Phone) English: 866-456-4995
             Espanol: 888-835-3505

Alabama Prison Project

619 N. Bridge Street
Wetumpka, AL 36092
(Phone) 334-264-7416
Email: halberet@mindspring.com

Alabama State Bar Volunteer Lawyers Program

415 Dexter Avenue
Montgomery, AL 36104
(Phone) 334-269-1803

Equal Justice Initiative

122 Commerce Street
Montgomery, AL 36104
(Phone) 334-269-1803
Website: www.eji.org
EJI litigates on behalf of condemned prisoners, juvenile offenders, people wrongly convicted or charged with violent crimes, poor people denied effective representation, and others whose trials are marked by racial bias or prosecutorial misconduct.

Legal Services Alabama

2567 Fairlane Drive, Ste. 200
Montgomery, AL 36116
(Phone) 334-832-4570

Legal Services Corporation of Alabama, Inc.

Tuscaloosa Regional Office
1351 McFarland Boulevard E., 11th Floor
Tuscaloosa, AL 35404
(Phone) 205-758-7503

Legal Services Corporation

P. O. Box 20787
Montgomery, AL 36120
(Phone) 866-456-4995

Southern Poverty Law Center

400 Washington Avenue
Montgomery, AL 36104
(Phone) 334-956-8200
Website: http://splcenter.org

ALASKA

ACLU of Alaska
P. O. Box 201844
Anchorage, AK 99520
(Phone) 907-276-2258
Email: akclu@akclu.org
Website: www.akclu.org

Alaska Disability Law Center
3330 Arctic Boulevard, Ste. 103
Anchorage, AK 99501
(Phone) 907-565-1001

Alaska Legal Services Corporation - Anchorage
1016 W. 4th Avenue, Ste. 200
Anchorage, AK 99501
(Phone) 907-272-9431
Email: anchorage3@alsc.law.org
Provides free civil (non-criminal) legal assistance to low-income Alaskans. Advocates reducing the legal consequences of poverty. We are sorry, but we cannot respond to requests for legal assistance made by email. Any information that you send to us by email is not confidential and is not protected by the attorney/client privilege. Referrals will be given if possible.

Alaska Legal Services Corporation – Bethel
P. O. Box 248
Bethel, AK 99559
(Phone) 907-543-2237
Email: bethel@alsc-law.org
Website: www.alaskalawhelp.org

Alaska Legal Services Corporation – Dillingham
P. O. Box 176
Dillingham, AK 99576
(Phone) 907-842-1452
Email: dillingham@alsc-law.org
Website: www.alaskalawhelp.org

Alaska Legal Services Corporation – Fairbanks

1648 Cushman, Ste. 300
Fairbanks, AK 99701
(Phone) 907-452-5181
Email: fairbanks@alsc-law.org
Website: www.alaskalawhelp.org

Alaska Legal Services Corporation – Juneau

419 6th Street, Ste. 322
Juneau, AK 99801
(Phone) 907-586-6425
Email: fairbanks@alsc-law.org
Website: www.alaskalawhelp.org

Alaska Legal Services Corporation – Ketchikan

306 Main Street, Ste. 218
Ketchikan, AK 99901
(Phone) 907-225-6420
Email: ketchikan@alsc-law.org
Website: www.alaskalawhelp.org

Alaska Legal Services Corporation – Kotzebue

P. O. Box 526
Kotzebue, AK 99901
(Phone) 907-225-6420
Email: kotzbue@alsc-law.org
Website: www.alaskalawhelp.org

Alaska Human Rights Commission

800 A Street, Ste. 204
Anchorage, AK 99501
(Phone) 907-274-4692
Website: http://gov.state.ak.us/aschr
Provides assistance and investigates discrimination and other human-rights abuses statewide.

Alaska Immigration Justice Project

431 West 7th Avenue, Ste. 208
Anchorage, AK 99501

Alaska Network on Domestic Violence and Sexual Assault

130 Seward Street, Ste. 214
Juneau, AK 99801
(Phone) 888-520-2666

Alaska Pro Bono Program
P. O. Box 140191
Anchorage, AK 99514-0191
(Phone) 907-272-9431

ARIZONA

ACLU of Arizona
P. O. Box 17148
Phoenix, AZ 85011
(Phone) 602-650-1967
Email: intake@acluaz.org
Website: www.acluaz.org

AIDS Project Arizona
1427 N. 3rd Street
Phoenix, AZ 85004
(Phone) 602-253-2437

Arizona Federal Public Defender's Office
222 N. Central Avenue, Ste. 810
Phoenix, AZ 85004
(Phone) 602-379-3670

American Friends Service Committee
103 N. Park Avenue
Tucson, AZ 85719
(Phone) 520-623-9141
Email: afscaz.org
Website: www.afsc.org/az
Serves as a resource for prisoners, ex-prisoners, and their family members to find information and resources to address their questions and needs, and a place to get involved in bringing their voices to the seats of power in Arizona.

Arizona Justice for Children
P. O. Box 45500
Phoenix, AZ 85064
(Phone) 602-235-9300

Hallinan & Killpack Law Firm
5240 E. Pima Street
Tucson, AZ 85712
(Phone) 520-320-5240x107
Website: www.hlfaz.com
Their focus areas are prison medical negligence and prison wrongful death due to medical negligence.
Handles only Arizona cases at this time.

HIV/AIDS Law Project
303 E. Palm Lane
Phoenix, AZ 85004
(Phone) 602-258-3434

Immigration Service
105 East Grant Road
Tucson, AZ 85705
(Phone) 520-620-9950

Middle Ground Prison Reform, Inc.
139 East Encanto Drive
Tempe, AZ 85281
(Phone) 480-966-8116
Email: middleground@msn.com
Website: www.middlegroundprisonreform.org
Provides education/training programs, counseling, legislative advocacy for prison reform litigation on
policies and procedures affecting visitors, public speaking on criminal and social justice issues,
referrals to social service agencies. Advocacy and public education is performed on state and
national levels. Direct services are provided statewide in Arizona.

Northern Arizona Justice Project
Department of Criminal Justice
Northern Arizona University
P.O. Box 15005
Flagstaff, AZ 86011-5005
(Phone) 928-523-7028
Website: http://Jan.ucc.nav.edu/d-najp

ARKANSAS

ACLU of Arkansas
904 West Second Street, Ste. #1
Little Rock, AR 72201
(Phone) 501-374-2660
Website: www.acluarkansas.org
Prison conditions, county jail conditions/treatment referrals, litigation, referrals to Compliance Coordinator.

Arkansas Volunteer Lawyers for the Elderly
2020 W. 3rd Street, Ste. 620
Little Rock, AR 72205
(Phone) 501-376-9263

Center for Arkansas Legal Services
1300 W. 6th Street
Little Rock, AR 72201
(Phone) 501-376-3423

Legal Aid of Arkansas
1200 Henryetta Street
Springdale, AR 72762
(Phone) 800-952-9243

Legal Services of Arkansas
615 West Markham Street, Ste. 200
Little Rock, AK 72201
(Phone) 501-376-8015

Midwest Innocence Project
605 West 47th Street
Kansas City, MO 64113
(Phone) 816-221-2166
Website: www.themip.org
The MIP is dedicated to the investigation, litigation, and exoneration of wrongfully convicted men and women in the following states: AR, KS, **MO**, IA, and NE

Women's Project

2224 Main Street
Little Rock, AR 72206
(Phone) 501-372-5113
Website: www.womens-project.org

All services are provided only in Arkansas at the state women's prison and community punishment center. They include a weekly battered women's support group, biweekly peer AIDS education program, a child transportation project, yearly caretakers' retreat. Provides prison library through donations or books and periodicals and support with job search for women parolees in Arkansas.

CALIFORNIA

ACLU of Northern California

39 Drumm Street
San Francisco, CA 94111
(Phone) 621-2493

ACLU of San Diego & Imperial Counties

P.O. Box 87131
San Diego, CA 92138-7131
(Phone) 619-232-2131
Email: info@aclusandiego.org
Website: www.aclusandiego.org

ACLU of Southern California

1616 Beverly Boulevard
Los Angeles, CA 90026
(Phone) 213-977-9543
Email: acluinfo@aclu-sc.org
L.A. County jail conditions; habeas corpus, post-conviction and prison conditions; referrals

Ahrony, Graham & Zucker, LLP

401 Wilshire Blvd., 12th Floor PH
Santa Monica, CA 90401
(Phone) 310-979-6400
Website: www.ahronygraham.com

This is an appellate and post-conviction law firm. They specialize in appeals, Habeas Corpus Writs (Factual Innocence), parole hearings, SB 260 hearings, MDO hearings, re-sentencing, probation violations, rap sheet correction, prison and parole issues, 115 discipline issues, for California and federal courts.

Asian Pacific Islander Legal Outreach
1121 Mission Street
San Francisco, CA 94103
(Phone) 415-567-6255

Bay Area Legal Aid
1735 Telegraph Avenue
Oakland, CA 94612
(Phone) 510-663-4755

Benjamin Ramos, Esquire
705 E. Bidwell, Ste. 2-359
Folsom, CA 95630
(Phone) 916-358-9842
Experienced habeas corpus lawyer admitted in all California State and Federal courts. Gives parole representation, challenges bogus gang validation, and more.

California Appellate Project
(Capital Cases ONLY!)
Attn: Michael G. Millman
1 Ecker Place, Ste. 400
San Francisco, CA 94105-2750
(Phone) 800-779-0507
           415-495-0500

California Center for Capital Assistance
Attn: Scharlette Holdman
529 Castro Street
San Francisco, CA 94114
(Phone) 415-621-8860

California Coalition for Women Prisoners
1540 Market Street, Ste. 490
San Francisco, CA 94102
(Phone) 415-255-7036 x4
Raise public consciousness about the cruel and inhumane conditions under which women in prison live and advocate for positive change. Promote the leadership of and give voice to women prisoners and former prisoners.

California State Public Defender
801 K Street, Ste. 1100
Sacramento, CA 95814
(Phone) 916-322-7442

California State Public Defender

221 Main Street, 10th Floor
San Francisco, CA 94105
(Phone) 415-904-5600

California Western School of Law Institute for Criminal Defense Advocacy

California Innocence Project
225 Cedar Street
San Diego, CA 92101
(Phone) 619-525-1485

Charles Carbone, Esquire

PMB 212
3128 16TH Street
San Francisco, CA 94103
Website: www.prisonerattorney.com

Defense Investigation Group

P.O. Box 86923
Los Angeles, CA 90086
Affordable investigation services. $500 post-conviction investigations, locates up to three people in Los Angeles/Orange counties.

Disability Rights Education Defense Fund

2212 6th Street
Berkeley, CA 94710
(Phone) 510-644-2555
Website: www.dredf.org
Provides legal referrals for prisoners with disability issues

Disability Rights Education and Defense Fund, Inc.

3075 Adeline Street, Ste. 210
Berkeley, CA 94703
CA Prisoners only. DREDF only takes on a few cases each year. "We receive far more requests for assistance than our resources allow us to take on. If we cannot take your case, we can provide you with referrals to other organizations."

Feria & Corona Law Firm

10 Universal City Plazas, Ste. 2000
Universal City, CA 91608
(Phone) 818-905-0903

Hopkins Law Office

140 B Street, #5-240
Davis, CA 95616
(Phone) 520-465-2658
Website: www.thehopkinslawoffice.com
Email: objectionyourhonor@hotmail.com
Licensed attorney for California and Arizona 9th Circuit and Supreme Court

Justice Now

1322 Webster Street, Ste. 210
Oakland, CA 94612
(Phone) 510-839-7654
Focuses solely on the needs of women prisoners. They work on alternative sentencing, document human rights abuses in prison, and building a World Without Prisons Project (works with women prisoners to get their words and art in the media).

LaRaza Centro Legal, Inc.

Lawyer Referral Service and Pro Bono Project
474 Valencia Street, Ste. 295
San Francisco, CA 94103-3415
This legal aid service is mainly for Spanish-speaking prisoners. They handle all types of legal problems, civil, criminal, parole, and post-conviction services. All attorneys are located in California but no geographic requirements for clients.

Law Office of Donald R. Hammond

222 W. 6th Street, Ste. 400
San Pedro, CA 90731
(Phone) 323-529-3660
Website: www.donhammondlaw.com
Attorney Don Hammond is a member of the Fair Chance Project.

Law Office of Stanley Goff

15 Boardman Place
San Francisco, CA 94103
(Phone) 415-571-9570
Email: scraiggoff@aol.com
Police misconduct, criminal defense (Prop 47 Petitions), personal injury, and all other Civil Rights violations.

Legal Aid – Central California Legal Services

2115 Kern Street, Ste. 200
Fresno, CA 93721
(Phone) 559-570-1200

Legal Insights, Inc.
25602 Alicia Parkway, Ste. 323
Laguna Hills, CA 92653
Website: www.infolegalinsights.com
Professional specialists with extensive post-conviction experience. They do just about every type of appeal, and they are a national service covering all 50 states! FREE initial consultation.

Northern California Innocence Project
Santa Clara Law: Santa Clara University
500 El Camino Road
Santa Clara, CA 95053
(Phone) 408-554-4361
Email: lawadmissions@scu.edu
The mission of the Northern California Innocence Project (NCIP) is to promote a fair, effective, and compassionate criminal justice system and protect the rights of the innocent.

NW Immigrant Rights Project
Eastern Washington Office
212 Sunnyside Avenue, Ste. 270
Granger, WA 98932
Website: www.nwirp.org
They promote justice for low-income immigrants by pursuing and defending their legal status. They also focus on direct legal services, supported by education and public policy work.

Penal Law Project
Community Legal Information Clinic
California State University
400 W. First Street, Room 121
Chico, CA 95929-0190
(Phone) 530-898-4354
Email: clic@csuchico.edu
Penal Law Project assists incarcerated individuals. The program's primary purpose is to provide legal information and research for those held in CA State prisons.

Prison Law Clinic
UC Davis School of Law
One Shields Avenue
Building TB30
Davis, CA 95616
(Phone) 530-752-6942
Email: mmmurphy@ucdavis.edu
Prison conditions, parole revocations, legal research. Services are provided to prisoners of California State Prisons.

Prison Law Office
General Delivery
San Quentin, CA 94964
(Phone) 415-457-9144
Website: www.prisonlaw.com
Provides direct legal assistance for the range of problems encountered by California prisoners, excluding attacks on criminal convictions. The focus is on conditions of confinement. Provides pamphlets pertaining to various problems free of charge to prisoners.

Prisoner Legal Services
1540 Market Street, Ste. 490
San Francisco, CA 94102
(Phone) 415-255-7036

Prison Law Clinic
UC Davis School of Law
One Shields Avenue, TB30
Davis, CA 95616
(Phone) 530-752-6942
Website: www.law.ucdavis.edu/faculty/Murphy
Their students provide legal services to clients incarcerated in state prison.

Prison Services
Marin County Jail
13 Peter Behr Drive
San Rafael, CA 94903
(Phone) 415-499-3203
Provides direct services for prisoners in the Marin County Jail and their families, including referrals to community agencies regarding counseling on drugs and alcohol dependency; food and clothing; literacy programs; family counseling; and orientation for prisoners and families moving on to state prisons. Excellent resource for San Quentin prisoners temporarily detained here.

Pro Bono Project
480 N. First Street
San Jose, CA 95112
(Phone) 408-998-5298

Public Interest Law Firm

111 West St. John Street, Ste. 315
San Jose, CA 95113
(Phone) 408-280-2417
A program of the Law Foundation of Silicon Valley, the mission is to protect human rights of individuals and groups in the Silicon Valley area who are underrepresented in the civil justice system. PILF accomplishes its mission by leveraging the skills and resources of pro bono attorneys to provide high quality representation in class action and impact litigation, advocacy in state and local government, and litigation support to local legal services programs.

State Public Defender – San Francisco

221 Main Street, 10th Floor
San Francisco, CA 94105
(Phone) 415-904-5600
Capital appeals (only) for convicted felony indigents.

The Action Committee for Women in Prison

769 Northwestern Drive
Claremont, CA 91711
(Phone) 626-710-7543
Website: www.acwip.net

William L. Schmidt, Esquire

P.O. Box 25001
Fresno, CA 93729
Email: 911civilrights@gmail.com
Legal services for California inmates: appeals; writ of habeas corpus; civil rights litigation; catastrophic injury/excessive force; money management; gang issues; transfers.

COLORADO

ACLU of Colorado

400 Corona Street
Denver, CO 80218
(Phone) 303-777-5482
Email: info@aclu-co.org
Website: www.aclu.org
Handles habeas corpus and prison-condition matters, damage suits. Provides direct referrals.

Colorado CURE

3470 S. Poplar, Ste. 406
Denver, CO 80224
(Phone) 303-758-3390
Email: dianne@coloradocure.org
Website: www.coloradocure.org
Works primarily through legislative channels to reduce crime through reform of the criminal justice system. Provides prisoners and their families with information about rehabilitative programs. Provides no legal services. Publishes quarterly newsletter.

Colorado Legal Services

603 Main Street
Alamosa, CO 81101
(Phone) 719-589-4993

Colorado Office of the Public Defender

Attn: David D. Wymore
110 16th Street, Ste. 800
Denver, CO 80202
(Phone) 303-620-4888

Empowerment Program

Attn: Kathy Howard
1600 York Street
Denver, CO 80206
(Phone) 303-320-1989
Email: kat-howard@empowermentprogram.org
Website: www.empowermentprogram.org
Provides education, employment assistance, health, housing referrals and support services to women who are in disadvantaged positions due to incarceration, poverty, homelessness, HIV/AIDS infection or involvement in the criminal justice system. Our goal is to decrease rates of recidivism by providing case management support services, basic skills education, housing and resource coordination that can offer viable alternatives to habits and choices that may lead to criminal behaviors.

Heart of the Rockies Bar Association Pro Bono Program

1604 H Street
Salida, CO 81201
(Phone) 719-539-4251

Legal Aid Foundation

1120 N. Lincoln Street, Ste. 701
Denver, CO 80203
(Phone) 303-863-9544

New Foundation Non-Violence Center

901 W. 14th Avenue. Ste. 7
Denver, CO 80204
(Phone) 303-825-2562
www.home.earthlink.net/~nfnc
Offers a one-to-one visitation program at the Denver County Jail that includes advocacy and informal counseling. Organizes intensive three-day Alternatives to Violence Project (AVP) workshops to some Colorado penal facilities and some community settings.

Northern Colorado Legal Services

P. O. Box 1904
Leadville, CO 80461
(Phone) 719-486-3238

Southern Colorado AIDS Project

1301 S. 5th Street
Colorado Springs, CO   80903
(Phone) 719-578-9092

CONNECTICUT

Connecticut Bar Association

538 Preston Avenue, 3rd Floor
Meriden, CT 06450

Connecticut Legal Services

16 Main Street, 2nd Floor
New Britain, CT 06051
(Phone) 860-225-8678

Connecticut Legal Services

62 Washington Street, 4th Floor
Middletown, CT 06457
(Phone) 860-344-0447

Connecticut Statewide Legal Services

425 Main Street, Ste. 2
Middletown, CT 06457-3371
(Phone) 800-453-3320

Connecticut Trial Services Unit

Attn: Patrick J. Culligan
1 Hartford Square West
Hartford, CT 06106
(Phone) 203-566-5328

Greater Hartford Legal Aid

999 Asylum Avenue
Hartford, CT 06105
(Phone) 860-541-5000

Innovative Sentencing Solutions

78 Deepwood Drive
Avon, CT 06001
(Phone) 860-922-7321
Website: www.innovativesentencing.com
They offer a variety of services for federal prisoners.

Statewide Legal Services of Connecticut

Toll Free 800-453-3320
www.ctlawhelp.org/en/self-help

DELAWARE

Catholic Charities Immigration Services – Kent County Office

2099 S. Dupont Highway, Ste. A
Dover, DE 19901
(Phone) 302-674-1600

Community Legal Aid Society, Inc.

(CLASI)
New Castle County:
100 W. 10th St., Suite 801
Wilmington, DE 19801
(Phone) 302-575-0660
       800-292-7980
       302-575-0666 Elder Law Program
       302-575-0690 Disabilities Program
       302-575-0696 (TTY)

(CLASI)
Kent County
840 Walker Road
Dover, DE 19904
(Phone) 302-674-8500
       800-537-8383

(CLASI)
Sussex County
Georgetown Professional Park
20151 Office Circle
Georgetown, DE 19947
       302-856-0038
       800-462-7070 (Toll Free)

Delaware Legal Aid Society

913 Washington Street
Wilmington, DE 19801
(Phone) 302-575-0660

Delaware State Bar Association Lawyer Referral Service

405 N. King Street, Ste. 100
Wilmington, DE 19803
(Phone) 800-773-0606

Delaware Volunteer Legal Services

4601 Concord Pike
Wilmington, DE 19803
(Phone) 302-478-8680
Website: www.dvls.org/

Office of the Public Defender
Carvel State Office Building
820 N. French Street, 3rd Floor
Wilmington, DE 19801
(Phone) 302-577-5200

Wilmington Community Legal Aid
100 W. 10th Street, Ste. 801
Wilmington, DE 19801
(Phone) 302-575-0660

FLORIDA

Executive Clemency
2112 SW 34th Street, Ste. 237
Gailnesville, FL 32608
(Phone) 954-271-2304
Website: www.nationalclemencyprojectinc.com. They offer information on sentence reduction through executive clemency. Over 35 years' experience of clemency, parole assistance, and transfers. Preparing application packets to be submitted on behalf of state and federal inmates.

Florida Bar
651 E. Jefferson Street
Tallahassee, FL
(Phone) 850-561-5600

Florida Capital Collateral Representatives
1533 South Monroe Street
Tallahassee, FL 32301
(Phone) 904-487-4326

Florida Justice Institute
3750 Miami Tower
100 S.E. Second Street
Miami, FL 33131-2309
(Phone) 305-358-2081
Website: www.floridajusticeinstitute.org

Habeas Assistance & Training Project
Attn: Mark E. Olive
1900 Center Point Boulevard, Suite 80
Tallahassee, FL 32308
(Phone) 904-877-7210

Hillsborough County Bar Association

1610 N Tampa Street
Tampa, FL 33602
(Phone) 813-221-7777

Innocence Project of Florida

1100 East Park Avenue
Tallahassee, FL 32301
(Phone) 850-561-6767
Website: www.floridainnocence.org
The Innocence Project of Florida (IPF) is a non-profit founded in 2003 to help innocent prisoners in Florida obtain their freedom and rebuild their lives.

Justice Solutions of America

P. O. Box 830293
Ocala, FL 34483
(Phone) 888-577-4766
Website: www.federalprisonconsultants.com
           www.stateprisonadvocates.com

Lawyer Referral Service

(Phone) 800-342-8011

Miami Law Innocence Clinic

1311 Miller Drive, A-312
Miami, FL
(Phone) 305-284-8115

Pro Immigration Lawyers

3637 Cortez Road W., Unit 104
Bradenton, FL 34210
(Phone) 941-782-8903

Volunteer Lawyers Program

800 Drew Street
Clearwater, FL 33755
(Phone) 727-461-4880

GEORGIA

AIM
765 McDaniel Street
Atlanta, GA 30310
(Phone) 404-658-9606
An advocacy group for incarcerated mothers. AIM can provide helpful information for all women in prison who have children but can only provide social services in the Atlanta area.

Georgia Innocence Project
2645 North Decatur Road
Decatur, GA 30033
(Phone) 404-373-4433
Website: www.ga-innocenceproject.org

Georgia Indigent Defense Counsel
Attn: Mike Mears
985 Ponce de Leon Avenue
Atlanta, GA 30306
(Phone) 404-894-2595

Georgia Legal Services Program
For current information, please contact their website:
Website: www.glan.org.

Georgia Resource Center
Attn: Steve Bayliss & Beth Wells
101 Marietta Tower, Ste. 3310
Atlanta, GA 30303
(Phone) 404-614-2014

Georgia Volunteer Lawyers for the Arts
675 Ponce de Leon Avenue NE
Atlanta, GA 30308
(Phone) 404-873-3911

Michael Maloof, Esquire
215 N. McDonough Street
Decatur, GA 30030
(Phone) 404-373-8000

National Association of Criminal Defense Attorneys
Attn: Renee McDonald
83 Poplar Street NW
Atlanta, GA 30303-2122
(Phone) 404-688-1202

State Bar of Georgia Pro Bono Project
104 Marietta Street NW, Ste. 100
Atlanta, GA 30303
(Phone) 404-527-8700

Southern Center for Human Rights
Contact: Tanya Greene
83 Poplar Street NW
Atlanta, GA 30303-2122
(Phone) 404-688-1201
Email: tgreene@schr.org

Thomas M. West, Attorney at Law
400 Colony Square, Ste. 200
1201 Peachtree Street NE
Atlanta, GA 30361
(Phone) 404-589-0136
Email: tom_mcwest@hotmail.com
Post-conviction, habeas corpus, prison conditions, direct referrals, damage suits, and criminal defense.

HAWAII

ACLU of Hawaii
P. O. Box 3410
Honolulu, HI 96801
(Phone) 808-522-5900
Email: office@acluhawaii.org
Website: www.acluhawaii.org
Handles prison conditions and individual abuse cases, limited to state prisons.

Community Alliance on Prisons
P. O. Box 37185
Honolulu, HI 96837

Foundation for Innocence

P.O. Box 1033
Kula, HI 96790
(Phone) 808-269-0452
Email: innocencehawaii@yahoo.com

Hawaii Innocence Project

Attn: Prof. Hench
University of Hawaii School of Law
2515 Dole Street
Honolulu, HI 96822
(Phone) 808-956-6547
Website: www.innocenceprojecthawaii.org
The Hawaii Innocence Project (HIP) provides FREE legal assistance to Hawaii prisoners with substantiated claims of actual innocence in seeking exoneration including investigating and obtaining DNA testing.

Legal Aid Society of Hawaii

1108 Nuuanu Avenue
Honolulu, HI 96817
(Phone) 808-536-4302

Office of the Ombudsman

ATTN: Robin K. Matsunga
465 S. King Street, 4th Floor
Honolulu, HI 96813
(Phone) 808-587-0770
Email: complaints@ombudsman.hawaii.gov
Receives complaints from prisoners regarding conditions of confinement at facilities operated by the State of Hawaii.

IDAHO

ACLU of Idaho

P.O. Box 1897
Boise, ID 83701
(Phone) 208-344-9750
Email: admin@acluidaho.org
Website: www.acluidaho.org
Advocates for civil liberties in Idaho including the rights of prisoners.

Durham Law Office

Craig H. Durham, Esquire
910 W. Main Street, Ste. 328
Boise, ID 83702
(Phone) 208-724-2617
Appeals, post-conviction, habeas, and parole services for Idaho inmates.

Executive Prison Consultants

2384 Oaktrail Drive, Ste. 2
Idaho Falls, ID 83404
Email: info@executiveprisonconsultants.com

Idaho Innocence Project

Boise State University
1910 University Drive
Boise, ID 83725
Focuses on cases where DNA evidence would change the outcome. Write for more criteria.

Idaho Legal Aid Services

310 North 5th Street
P. O. Box 913
Boise, ID 83701-0913
(Phone) 208-336-8980

ILLINOIS

ACLU of Illinois

180 N. Michigan Avenue, Ste. 2300
Chicago, IL 60601-7401
(Phone) 312-201-9740
Email: acluofillinois@aclu-il.org
Website: www.aclu-il.org

Chicago Innocence Project

205 West Monroe Street, Ste. 315
Chicago, IL 60606
(Phone) 312-263-6213
The Chicago Innocence Project investigates cases in which prisoners may have been convicted of crimes they did not commit, with priority to murder cases that resulted in sentences of death or life without parole.

Cook County Public Defender Capital Defense List
2650 South Carolina Street, 7th Floor
Chicago, IL 60608
(Phone) 312-814-5100

Illinois CURE
Attn: Dr. Maria Rudisch
3134 E. 92nd Street
Chicago, IL 60617
(Phone) 773-933-7919

Institute of Women Today
7315 S. Yale Avenue
Chicago, IL 60621
(Phone) 773-651-8372
Email: IWT7315@aol.com
Civil-rights actions, habeas corpus, direct referrals, legal research, prison health care, employment and vocational guidance, skills training, counseling, advocates for children of incarcerated mothers. We also have two shelters for former female prison residents and their children in Chicago: Maria Shelter (transitional shelter with 4-month stay) and Casa Notre Dame (second-stage shelter with maximum 2-year stay for women who need more time to accomplish their goals).

Illinois Innocence Project
University of Illinois Springfield
One University Plaza
Springfield, IL 62703-5407
(Phone) 217-206-6600

Jewish Prisoners Assistance Foundation
9401 N. Margail
Des Plains, IL 60016
(Phone) 847-296-1770
Website: www.chabadandfree.com
Helps protect the rights of Jewish prisoners in Illinois. Pre-and post-release counseling with prisoners and their families and support programs to obtain housing and employment for ex-offenders.

John Howard Associates

300 West Adams Street, Ste. 423
Chicago, IL 60606
(Phone) 312-782-1901; 312-782-1902 fax
Email: info@john-howard.org
Website: www.john-howard.org
Services: Limited direct services within Illinois, monitoring of Illinois prisons and jails and advocacy on prison conditions and prisoners' rights.

MacArthur Justice Center

Attn: Locke Bowman
Northwestern University School of Law
375 E. Chicago Avenue
Chicago, IL 60611
(Phone) 312-503-1271
Does impact litigation on criminal justice issues, especially prison conditions. While we do conduct litigation on behalf of prisoners, we do not accept all cases. Services for federal and state prisoners.

People's Law Office

1180 North Milwaukee Avenue
Chicago, IL 60642-4019
(Phone) 773-235-0070
Website: www.peopleslawoffice

The Exoneration Project

312 North May Street, Ste. 100
Chicago, IL 60607
(Phone) 312-789-4955
Website: www.exonerationproject.org
The Exoneration Project is a non-profit organization dedicated to working to FREE prisoners who were wrongfully convicted. The project represents innocent individuals in post-conviction proceedings.

Transformative Justice Law Project of Illinois

4707 North Broadway, Ste. 307
Chicago, IL 60640
(Phone) 773-272-1822
Provides legal services to transgender and gender nonconforming people targeted by the criminal legal system.

Law Office of Matthew S. Pinix

1200 East Capital Drive., Ste. 360
Milwaukee, WI 53211
(Phone) 414-963-6164
Website: www.pinixlawoffice.com

Specializes in criminal appeal cases and civil rights. They handle direct appeal, post-conviction, and habeas cases in the States of **Wisconsin** and **Illinois** only.

INDIANA

ACLU Indiana

1031 E. Washington Street
Indianapolis, IN 46202
(Phone) 317-635-4056
Website: www.aclu-in.org

Indiana CURE

P. O. Box 199256
Indianapolis, IN 46219
(Phone) 317-357-2606
Email: director@incure.org

Indiana Legal Services Support

151 North Delaware Street, 18th Floor
Indianapolis, IN 46204
(Phone) 317-631-9410

Public Defender of Indiana

1 N. Capitol, Ste. 800
Indianapolis, IN 46204
(Phone) 317-232-2475

Provides legal representation to indigent prisoners in post-conviction actions challenging Indiana convictions/sentences in state court *only*. Represents juveniles in parole revocation proceedings. Also accepts appointment at county expense for trial or appeal.

Wrongful Conviction Clinic

Indiana University School of Law
530 W. New York Street, Room 111
Indianapolis, IN 46202-3225
(Phone) 317-274-5551
Cases accepted: Cases of actual innocence in Indiana; DNA and non-DNA cases; will consider arson, shaken baby syndrome, and child abuse cases.

IOWA

ACLU Iowa

901 Insurance Exchange Building
Des Moines, IA 50309
(Phone) 515-243-3576
Website: www.iowaclu.org

Innocence Project of Iowa

19 South 7th Street
Estherville, IA 51334
Website: www.iowa.innocence.org

Iowa Citizens' Aide Ombudsman

Attn: William Angrick
Ola Babcock Miller Building
1112 E. Grand Avenue, 1st Floor, W. Wing
Des Moines, IA 50319
(Phone) 515-281-3592
Handles issues related to prisons, jails, and the Iowa Department of Corrections

Iowa CURE

P. O. Box 41005
Des Moines, IA 50311-4718
(Phone) 515-277-6296
Works toward reform of sentencing laws, including clemency procedure and sentence length, assists in job training and enhancement of prison-family relationships.

Legal Services Corporation of Iowa

312 8th Street, Ste. 300
Des Moines, IA 50309-3828
(Phone) 515-243-2151

University of Iowa College of Law – Legal Clinic
Attn: John Whiston
University of Iowa College of Law
Iowa City, IA 52242
(Phone) 319-335-9023
Email: law-legal-clinic@uiowa.edu
Handles post-convictions, habeas corpus and prison-condition cases and provides direct referrals. Maintains a waiting list in order to limit the number of cases assigned to students. Legal research is subject to delays. Services limited to prisoners in Iowa or serving Iowa sentences in other jurisdictions.

KANSAS

ACLU of Kansas and Western Missouri
3601 Main Street
Kansas City, MO 64111
(Phone) 816-756-3113
Website: www.aclukswmo.org
Handles prison-conditions cases and provides direct referrals, does not handle post-conviction matters.

Kansas Legal Services
400 State Avenue, Suite 1015
Kansas City, KS 66101
(Phone) 913-621-0200
Website: www.kansaslegalservices.org

Kansas Legal Services, Inc.
712 South Kansas Avenue, Ste. 200
Topeka, KS 66603
(Phone) 913-223-2068

Paul E. Wilson Defender Project
Attn: Jean K. Gilles Phillips
University of Kansas, School of Law
409 Green Hall
Lawrence, KS 66045
(Phone) 785-864-5572
Handles post-conviction and habeas corpus cases; only provides advice on civil matters. Assists prisoners in Kansas and Leavenworth Federal Penitentiary.

KENTUCKY

ACLU of Kentucky
315 Guthrie Street, Ste. 300
Louisville, KY 40202
(Phone) 502-581-1181
Email: info@aclu-ky.org

Federal Death Penalty Resource Counsel
Attn: Kevin McNally
P. O. Box 1243
Frankfort, KY 40602
(Phone) 502-227-2142

Jefferson County Public Defender
Attn: Daniel T. Goyette
719 West Jefferson, 200 Civic Plaza
Louisville, KY 40202
(Phone) 502-574-3800

Kentucky Capital Post-Conviction Unit
Attn: Randall Wheeler
100 Fair Oaks Lane, Ste. 302
Frankfort, KY 40601
(Phone) 502-564-3948

Kentucky Department of Public Advocacy
Attn: Allison Conally
100 Fair Oaks Lane, Ste. 302
Frankfort, KY 40601
(Phone) 502-564-8006

Kentucky Innocence Project
Department of Public Advocacy
 100 Fair Oaks Lane, Ste. 302
Frankford, KY 40601
(Phone) 502-564-3948
Website: www.dpa.ky.gov/kip

Medical Malpractice

106 Mayfield Avenue
South Shore, KY 41175
Email: baddocs2015@gmail.com

Office of Kentucky Legal Service

201 West Short Street, Ste. 506
Lexington, KY 40507
(Phone) 606-233-3057

LOUISIANA

ACLU of Louisiana

P. O. Box 56157
(Phone) 504-522-0617
Email: admin@laaclu.org
Website: www.laaclu.org
Provides post-conviction referrals. Consider prison conditions and civil rights violations for impact litigation.

Juvenile Justice Project of Louisiana

1600 Oretha C. Haley Boulevard
New Orleans, LA 70113
(Phone) 504-522-5437
Website: www.jjpl.org
Provides legal services for juveniles.

Louisiana Crisis Assistance Center

Attn: Clive Stafford Smith
636 Baronne Street
New Orleans, LA 70113
(Phone) 504-558-9867

Louisiana CURE

P. O. Box 181
Baton Rouge, LA 70821
Website: www.jjpl.org
Provides legal services for juveniles.

Loyola Death Penalty Resource Center

Attn: Nicholas Trenticosta
636 Baronne Street
New Orleans, LA 70113
(Phone) 504-522-0578

MAINE

ACLU Maine

401 Cumberland Avenue, Ste. 105
Portland, ME 04101
(Phone) 207-774-5444
Email: info@mclu.org
Website: www.mclu.org

Cumberland Legal Aid Clinic

Attn: Diane Arbour
University of Maine School of Law
246 Deering Avenue
Portland, ME 04102
(Phone) 207-780-4370
Website: www.mainelaw.maine.edu/cumberlandlegal.aspx
Provides legal representation for low-income individuals in Cumberland, York, and Southern Androscoggin. Assists in civil cases including divorce, parental rights and responsibilities, general civil litigation, civil rights litigation, and non-fee generating tort litigation. Provides criminal defense for any class of crime at the state level and in the U.S. District Court for the District of Maine. Also, protection from abuse and harassment litigation in all service areas. Clients are represented by seniors in law school who are specially licensed to practice law in the State of Maine.

Maine CURE

6 Boulder Lane
Lyman, ME 04002
(Phone) 207-449-7334

NDRAN CURE

(National Death Row Assistance Network)
6 Tolman Road
Peaks Island, ME 04108
(Phone) 207-766-2418
Email: claudia@ndran.org
Website: www.ndran.org

MARYLAND

ACLU of Maryland
3600 Clipper Mill Road, Ste. 350
Baltimore, MD 21211
(Phone) 410-889-8555
Email: aclu@aclu-md.org
Handles prison conditions cases. Direct representation by the ACLU is available only in cases involving violation of constitutional rights. The Baltimore office also handles all cases concerning prisoners in Eastern Shore jails.

Alternative Directions, Inc.
2505 N. Charles Street
Baltimore, MD 21218
(Phone) 410-889-5072
Alternative Directions provides free legal assistance to persons in prison or recently released from incarceration. Most cases handled involve family and domestic legal issues. The program also provides monthly workshops to prisoners on legal rights and responsibilities.

Health Education Resource Organization
(HERO)
1734 Maryland Avenue
Baltimore, MD 21201
(Phone) 410-685-1180
Website: http://hero.mcrc.org
Sponsors volunteers who go to the Maryland State Penitentiary to provide counseling, facilitating meetings, contacting families and lawyers, distribute some literature and videos related to health issues. Contact them for specifics.

Maryland CURE
P. O. Box 1583
Annapolis, MD 21404
(Phone) 301-869-8180
Email: mdcure@curenational.org
Website: www.curenational.org/mdcure
Promotes and provides information about rehabilitative programs. Advocate for sensible use of prison space, alternatives to incarceration, and resources and programs that will assist prisoners. Local and National CURE newsletters available with an MD CURE membership.

Maryland Public Defender, Capital Defense Division
520 West Fayette Street
Baltimore, MD 21201
(Phone) 301-333-4840

Office of the Public Defender, Collateral Review Division

300 W. Preston Street, Ste. 213
Baltimore, MD 21201
(Phone) 410-767-8460
Website: www.opd.state.md.us
Handles post-convictions, parole revocation, and extradition matters for prisoners throughout Maryland. Services limited to Maryland state prisoners only.

Innocence Project of New Orleans

4051 Ulloa Street
New Orleans, LA 70119
Email: info@ip-no.org
Website: www.ip-no.org

MASSACHUSETTS

ACLU of Massachusetts

211 Congress Street
Boston, MA 02110
Email: info@aclum.org
Website: www.aclu-mass.org

CPCS Innocence Program

Attn: Lisa Kavanaugh, Program Director
21 McGrath Highway, 2nd Floor
Somerville, MA 02143
(Phone) 617-623-0591
Website: www.publiccounsel.net
The purpose of the CPCS Innocence Program is to obtain exonerations for indigent Massachusetts State defendants who are actually innocent of the crimes for which they have been convicted.

Harvard Prison Legal Assistance Project

(PLAP)
Attn: Pamela Cameron
Gannett House 100
Harvard Law School
Cambridge, MA 02138
(Phone) 617-495-3969 (non-collect)
(Hotline) 617-495-3127 (in-state prisoners only)
Representation of prisoners at disciplinary and/or parole hearings.

Michael P. DeMarco

Attorney at Law
146 Elm Street
Westfield, MA 01085
(Phone) 413-562-5400

New England Innocence Project

160 Boylston Street
Boston, MA 02116
(Phone) 857-277-7858

Prisoners' Legal Services

Ten Winthrop Square, 3rd Floor
Boston, MA 02110
(Phone) 617-482-2773
Website: http://plsma.org
Formerly the Massachusetts Correctional Legal Service.

MICHIGAN

Michigan Legal Services

220 Bagley Avenue, Ste. 900
Detroit, MI 48226
(Phone) 313-964-4130

Prison Legal Services of Michigan

209 E. Washington Avenue
Jackson, MI 49201
(Phone) 517-780-6639
Website: www.prisoneradvocacy.org

Thomas M. Cooley Innocence Project

300 S. Capital Avenue
P.O. Box 13038
Lansing, MI 48901
(Phone) 517-371-5140

MINNESOTA

ACLU of Minnesota
450 N. Syndicate Avenue, Ste. 230
St. Paul, MN 55104
Email: support@aclu-mn.org
Website: www.aclu.mn.org

Battered Women's Justice Project
1801 Nicollet Avenue South, Suite 102
Minneapolis, MN 55403
(Phone) 800-903-0111, ext. 01
Website: www.bwjp.org
Provides assistance/info to battered women charged with crimes and to their defense teams.

Innocence Project of Minnesota
Hamline University School of Law
1536 Hewitt Avenue
St. Paul, MN 55104
(Phone) 651-523-3152

Legal Assistance to Minnesota Prisoners
Attn: Brad Colbert
LAMP Clinic
875 Summit Avenue
St. Paul, MN 55105
(Phone) 651-290-8651
Provides civil legal services to persons incarcerated in Minnesota state prisons who can't afford or in any manner obtain a private attorney.

Legal Rights Center
Community Worker
1611 Park Avenue South
Minneapolis, MN 55404
(Phone) 612-337-0030
Email: office@legalrightscenter.org
Website: www.legalrightscenter.org
Handles post-conviction, direct referrals, and criminal defense cases only. No appeals except for cases previously handled by the Center.

Minnesota Legal Services Coalition
46 East 4th Street, Ste. 900
St. Paul, MN 55101
(Phone) 612-228-9105

Pro Bono Assistance in Minnesota
33 South Sixth Street, Ste. 4540
Minneapolis, MN 55402
(Phone) 612-333-1183

Pro Bono Assistance in Minnesota
332 Minnesota Street, Ste. 2550
St. Paul, MN 55101
(Phone) 612-333-1183

MISSISSIPPI

ACLU of Mississippi
P. O. Box 2242
Jackson, MS 39225-2242
(Phone) 601-355-6464
Email: msacluoffice@msaclu.org
Website: www.msaclu.org

Mississippi CURE
P. O. Box 1620
Philadelphia, MS 39350
Email: jonathan@mississippicure.org

Mississippi Innocence Project
University of Mississippi School of Law
P. O. Box 1848
University, MS 38677
(Phone) 662-915-5206

Mississippi Legal Services Coalition
775 North President Street, Ste. 300
Jackson, MS 39205
(Phone) 601-944-0765

MISSOURI

ACLU of Eastern Missouri
454 Whittier Street
St. Louis, MO 63108
(Phone) 314-652-3111
Pursues prison condition issues and provides research, information, and referrals to prisoners.

Agape House
Attn: Linda Lamb, Manager
810 East High
Jefferson City, MO 65101
(Phone) 573-636-5737
Provides overnight lodging for family and friends visiting inmates in prison areas. Also provides family-unification support.

Death Penalty Litigation Clinic
6155 Oak Street, Ste. 401
St. Louis, MO 63103
(Phone) 816-363-2795

Legal Services of Eastern Missouri
(LSEM)
(Main Office, St. Louis)
701 Market St., Ste. 1100
St. Louis, MO 63101
(Phone) 314-534-4200
　　　　 800-444-0514
Website: www.lsem.org

Midwest Innocence Project
605 West 47th Street
Kansas City, MO 64113
(Phone) 816-221-2166
Website: www.themip.org
The MIP is dedicated to the investigation, litigation, and exoneration of wrongfully convicted men and women in the following states: AR, KS, **MO**, IA, and NE

Missouri Bar Association
326 Monroe Street
Jefferson City, MO 65101
(Phone) 573-635-4128
Website: http://www.mobarprobono.org/Home.aspx

Missouri Public Defender, Capital Litigation Division
Attn: Karen Kraft
1221 Locust Street, Ste. 401
St. Louis, MO 63103
(Phone) 314-421-1058

Prisoner Family Services
Attn: Susan Smith
3540 Marcus Avenue
St. Louis, MO 63115
(Phone) 314-807-4352
Provides transportation once or twice per month to 19 Missouri correctional centers. Also provides overnight lodging, information, referrals, gifts for children, and public education and advocacy.

4-H Living Interactive Family Education
Missouri Department of Corrections
Institutional Activities Coordinator
11593 State Highway O
Mineral Point, MO 63660
(Phone) 573-438-6000 x1534
Provides enhanced visiting, parenting education and group activities to incarcerated individuals and their families at Potosi Correctional Center. Program uses National 4-H organizational framework.

MONTANA

ACLU of Montana
P.O. Box 1317
Helena, MT 59624
(Phone) 406-443-8590
Email: aclu@aclumontana.org

Helena Legal Services Association
616 Helena Avenue, Ste. 100
Helena, MT 59601
(Phone) 1-800-666-6899

Montana Innocence Project
P.O. Box 7607
Missoula, MT 59807
(Phone) 406-243-6698

Montana Legal Services Association
801 North Last Chance Gulch
Helena, MT 59601
(Phone) 406-442-9830

NEBRASKA

ACLU of Nebraska
941 O Street, Ste. 706
Lincoln, NE 68508
(Phone) 402-476-8091
Email: info@aclunebraska.org
Website: www.aclunebraska.org
Handles civil rights actions and habeas corpus. Cases are limited to constitutional issues. Provides direct referrals.

Legal Aid of Nebraska
209 S 19th Street, Ste. 200
Omaha, NE
(Phone) 402-348-1069
Website: legalaidofnebraska.org

Nebraska Center for Legal Services
1616 L Street
Lincoln, NE 68501
(Phone) 402-477-6680

Nebraska Innocence Project
P.O. Box 24183
Omaha, NE 68124-0183

NEVADA

ACLU of Nevada
732 South 6th Street, Ste. 200A
Las Vegas, NV 89101
(Phone) 702-366-1226
Email: aclunv@aclunv.org
Website: www.aclunv.org
Handles habeas corpus and prison-and-jail conditions cases. All services depend on the availability of volunteer counsel.

Jeffrey S. Banks, Esquire
485 West 5th Street
Reno, NV 89503
(Phone) 775-324-6640
Post-conviction filings, appeals, writs, petitions, placement, immigration removal, and more

Legal Aid Center of Southern Nevada
725 E. Charleston Blvd.
Las Vegas, NV 89104

Nevada Appellate & Post-Conviction Project
Attn: Michael Pescetta
330 South 3rd Street, Ste. 700
Las Vegas, NV 89101
(Phone) 702-388-6577, ext. 279

Northern Nevada Volunteer Attorneys for Rural Nevadans
(VARN)
412 West John Street, Ste. C
Carson City, NV 89703
(Phone) 775-883-8278
              866-448-8276

NEW HAMPSHIRE

ACLU of New Hampshire
18 Low Avenue
Concord, NH 03301
(Phone) 603-225-3080
Handles prison conditions, First Amendment, and prisoners' rights cases.

603 Legal Aid
93 North State Street, Ste. 200
Concord, NH 03301
(Phone) 603-224-3333

New Hampshire Legal Assistance
117 N. State Street
Concord, NH 03301
(Phone) 603-224-4107

NEW JERSEY

ACLU of New Jersey
P. O. Box 32159
Newark, NJ 07102
(Phone) 973-642-2084
Email: info@aclu-nj.org
Website: www.aclu-nj.org
Legal defense of serious violations of constitutional rights. Violations must originate within the State of New Jersey.

Garden State CURE
c/o Office of Jail & Prison Ministry
P. O. Box 5147
Trenton, NJ 08638
(Phone) 609-406-7400, x5655
Email: rschul@dioceseoftrenton.org

Innocence Project for Justice
(New Jersey cases)
Rutgers University School of Law Constitutional Litigation Clinic
123 Washington Street
Newark, NJ 07102

New Jersey Association on Correction
(NJAC)
986 S. Broad Street
Trenton, NJ 08611
(Phone) 609-396-8900
Provides direct services to offenders and ex-offenders and advocates to improve the criminal justice system. Direct services are offered through two pre-release facilities, Clinton House and Bates House. The two resource centers serve probationers and parolees. Residential facilities are restricted to state prisoners on community release. It also publishes *News and Views*, a quarterly newsletter discussing criminal justice and corrections issues available as a membership benefit. Membership is free to prisoners and $20 per year for non-prisoners.

New Jersey Public Defender, Appellate Section
31 Clinton Street
P.O. Box 46003
Newark, NJ 07101
(Phone) 973-877-1200

Statewide Pro Bono Coordinator Mercer
Mercer County Criminal Courthouse
400 South Warren Street, Ste. 109
Trenton, NJ 08650-0068

The Last Resort Innocence Project
Seton Hall University School of Law
1109 Raymond Blvd.
Newark, NJ 07102
(Phone) 973-642-8500

NEW MEXICO

Innocence and Justice Project
University of New Mexico School of Law
1117 Stanford NE
Albuquerque, NM 87131-0001
(Phone) 505-277-2671

New Mexico Legal Aid
505 Marquette Avenue NW
Albuquerque, NM 87102
(Phone) 505-243-7871

New Mexico Legal Services Support
121 Tijeras Avenue NE, Ste. 3100
Albuquerque, NM 87102-3400
(Phone) 505-243-7871

State Bar of New Mexico
5121 Masthead Street NE
Albuquerque, NM 87109
(Phone) 505-797-6000
        800-876-6227

NEW YORK

Alba Morales
Florida Direct File Project
Human Rights Watch
350 5th Avenue, 33rd Floor
New York, NY 10118
Were you under 18 at the time of your offense? Were you prosecuted in adult court in Florida? Human Rights Watch is conducting an investigation on how Florida prosecutors use Direct File and how this process affects juveniles. If your case got to adult court in Florida via Direct File, contact this person.

American Civil Liberties Union
125 Broad Street, 18th Floor
New York, NY 10004

Bukh Law Firm, PC
14 Wall Street
New York, NY 10005
(Phone) 212-729-1632
www.nyccriminallawyer.com

Elmer Robert Keach, III, P.C.
1040 Riverfront Center
P.O. Box 70
Amsterdam, NY 12010
(Phone) 518-434-1718
Website: www.keachlawfirm.com
This experienced civil rights attorney is dedicated to seeking justice for those who are incarcerated, offers affordable hourly rates for criminal defense, appeals, post-conviction relief, and habeas corpus.

Herbert Lehman Education Fund
Attn: George Kendall
99 Hudson Street, Ste. 1600
New York, NY 10013
(Phone) 212-219-1900
Non-profit law firm that deals only with cases of obvious race discrimination. They handle a small number of death penalty and life without parole cases.

Innocence Project
(National)
40 Worth Street, Ste. 701
New York, NY 10013

Legal Action Center

225 Varick Street. 4th Floor
New York, NY 10014
(Phone) 800-223-4044
Non-profit organization providing FREE legal services to formerly incarcerated people, recovering alcoholics, substance abusers, and people with HIV.

Legal Aid Society Prisoner's Rights Project

199 Water Street
New York, NY 10038
(Phone) 212-577-3300

MNN, Inc.

Shani Burton, Esquire
244 5th Avenue. Ste. B-230
New York, NY 10001

New York Capital Defender Office, Albany Office

Attn: Randolph Treece
Corning Tower
P. O. Box 2113
Albany, NY 12220
(Phone) 518-473-9429

New York Capital Defender, Rochester Office

Attn: Tom Dunn
277 Alexander Street, Ste. 201
Rochester, NY 14607
(Phone) 716-232-5480

New York Capital Defender Office

Attn: Kevin M. Doyle
80 Centre Street, Room 266
New York, NY 10013
(Phone) 212-417-3187

New York State Prisoner Justice Coalition

33 Central Avenue
Albany, NY 12210

Pace Post-Conviction Project
Barbara Salken Criminal Justice Clinic
78 North Broadway
White Plains, NY 10603
(Phone) 914-422-4230

Prisoners' Legal Services of New York
41 State Street, Ste. M112
Albany, NY 12207
(Phone) 518-445-6053
Website: www.plsny.org

Reinvestigation Project
Office of the Appellate Defender
11 Park Place, Ste. 1601
New York, NY 10007
(Phone) 212-402-4100

Sylvia Rivera Law Project
147 West 24th Street, 5th Floor
New York, NY 10001
(Phone) 212-337-8550
Provides FREE legal services to transgender and gender nonconforming low-income people and
people of color. Only available in New York and surrounding areas.

The Exoneration Initiative
233 Broadway, Ste. 2370
New York, NY 10279
(Phone) 212-965-9335
Website: www.exonerationinitiative.org

The Legal Aid Society
Attn: Russell Neufeld
175 Remsen Street
Brooklyn, NY 11201
(Phone) 718-243-6473

NORTH CAROLINA

ACLU of North Carolina
P. O. Box 28004
Raleigh, NC 27611
(Phone) 919-834-3390
Email: aclunc@nc.rr.com
Website: www.acluofnorthcarolina.org
Handles habeas corpus and prison-conditions cases. Provides direct referrals, including referrals for damage suits.

American Civil Liberties Union
Capital Punishment Project
201 West Main Street, Ste. 402
Durham, NC 27701
(Phone) 919-682-5659
Partnering with ACLU affiliates in death penalty states and with coalition partners nationally, CPP promotes both abolition and systemic reform of the death penalty.

North Carolina Center on Actual Innocence
P.O. Box 52446
Shannon Plaza Station
Durham, NC 27717
(Phone) 919-489-3218

North Carolina Center for Death Penalty Litigation
Attn: Kenneth Rose
200 Meredith Drive, Ste. 201
Durham, NC 27713
(Phone) 919-544-4650

North Carolina Prisoner Legal Services, Inc.
Brenda Richardson
P. O. Box 25397
Raleigh, NC 919-856-2200
Website: www.ncpls.org
Legal services to North Carolina Prisoners only. Provides a range of services from advice about prisoners' legal rights to representation in all state and federal courts. Handles a variety of legal matters involving prison conditions and criminal convictions. Write NCPLA for a brochure detailing which types of cases receive top priority, providing information on how to request assistance from NCPLS, and listing information packets and legal forms available to prisoners.

Prison-Ashram Project

c/o Human Kindness Foundation
P. O. Box 61619
Durham, NC 27715
(Phone) 919-383-5160
Website: www.humankindness.org

Project for Older Prisoners

2000 H Street NW
Washington, DC 20052
(Phone) 202-994-7001
Through George Washinton University Law School, law students interview and evaluate older and geriatric Inmates in obtaining parole or other forms of release from incarceration. Operates in six states: LA, MD, MI, **NC,** VA, and DC.

NORTH DAKOTA

ACLU of the Dakotas

112 North University Drive, Ste. 301
Fargo, ND 58102
(Phone) 701-461-7290
Email: info@acludakotas.org
Website: www.acludakotas.org

Legal Assistance of North Dakota

1025 North 3rd Street
PO Box 2419
Bismark, ND 58502-1893
(Phone) 701-222-2110

Legal Services of North Dakota

345 Main Street
New Town, ND 58763
(Phone) 800-634-5263
Website: www.lsnd.org

State Bar Association of North Dakota

1661 Capitol Way, Ste 104LL
Bismarck, ND 58501
(Phone) 701-255-1404
        800-472-2685

OHIO

Ohio Lawyers Assistance Program
Counseling & mental health in Columbus, United States
1650 Lake Shore Drive, Ste. 375
Columbus, OH 43204
(Phone) 800-348-4343
Website: www.ohiolap.org

Ohio Public Defender, Capital Punishment Division
8 East Long Street
Columbus, OH 43215
(Phone) 614-466-5394

Pro Bono Partnership of Ohio
312 N. Patterson Blvd
Dayton, OH 45402
(Phone) 937-396-2131

Wrongful Conviction Project
Office of the Ohio Public Defender
250 East Broad Street, Ste. 1400
Columbus, OH 43215
(Phone) 614-466-5394
Website: www.opd.ohio.gov/DP_wrongfulconviction

OKLAHOMA

ALCU of Oklahoma
3000 Paseo Drive
Oklahoma City, OK 73103
(Phone) 405-524-8511
Email: acluok@acluok.org
Website: www.acluok.org
Handles prison conditions cases and civil liberties situations. Provides limited referrals.

Human Services Department
940 NE 13th Street
Oklahoma City, OK 73104
(Phone) 405-271-3325
Website: www.oklahoma.gov

Oklahoma CURE
P. O. Box 9741
Tulsa, OK 74157-0741
(Phone) 918-744-9857
Email: okcure@earthlink.net
Website: www.home.earthlink.net/okcure

Oklahoma Human Services
2400 N. Lincoln Boulevard
Oklahoma City, Ok 73105
(405) 522-5050
 Website: www.OKDHS.org

Oklahoma Indigent Defense System, Cap P-Con Division
Attn: Sue Wycoff
1660 Cross Center Drive
Norman, OK 73019
(Phone) 405-325-3331

Oklahoma Innocence Project
2501 N. Blackwelder
Oklahoma City, OK 73106
(Phone) 405-208-6161
Email: innocence@okcu.edu

Oklahoma Legal Services Center
110 Cameron Building, 2915 Classen Blvd.
Oklahoma City, OK 73106
(Phone) 405-557-1940

OREGON

ACLU of Oregon
P. O. Box 40585
Portland, OR 97204-0585
(Phone) 503-227-3186
Email: info@aclu-or.org
Website: www.aclu-or.org
Handles limited post-conviction, habeas corpus, and prison condition cases. Direct referrals are provided to agencies but not to private attorneys.

Center for Nonprofit Legal Services
225 Main Street
Medford, OR 97501
(Phone) 541-779-7291

Center on Juvenile and Criminal Justice
(CJC)
Northwest Regional Office
Western Oregon University
HHS 223A
345 N. Monmouth
Monmouth, OR 97361
(Phone) 503-838-8401
Promotes balanced and humane criminal justice policies that reduce incarceration and promote long-term public safety for juveniles through the development of model programs, technical assistance, research/policy analysis, and public education.

Community Court Project
Multnomah County Adult Community Justice Offices
421 Southwest Fifth Avenue, Ste. 600
Portland, OR 97204
(Phone) 503-988-3007

Federal Public Defender, District of Oregon
(Main Office, Portland)
101 SW Main Street, Ste. 1700
Portland, OR 97204
(Phone) 503-326-2123

Federal Public Defender, District of Oregon

(Eugene Office)
151 W. 7th Street, Suite 510
Eugene, OR 97401
(Phone) 541-465-6937

Federal Public Defender, District of Oregon

(Medford Office)
15 Newton Street
Medford, OR 97502
(Phone) 541-776-3630

Lane County Law and Advocacy Center

376 East 11th Avenue
Eugene, OR 97401
(Phone) 541-485-1017

Legal Aid Services of Oregon

832 Klamath Avenue
Klamath Falls, OR 97601
(Phone) 541-273-0533

Marion-Polk Legal Aid

1655 State Street
Salem, OR 97301
(Phone) 530-581-5265

Oregon Legal Services Corporation

516 ES Morrison, Ste. 1000
Portland, OR 97214-2340
(Phone) 503-234-1534

The Portia Project

P.O. Box 3567
Eugene, OR 97403
(Phone) 541-255-9988
Website: www.theportiaproject.com
They provide legal and other assistance to women incarcerated at Coffee Creek Correctional Facility and women who are under post-prison supervision throughout the state.

PENNSYLVANIA

American Civil Liberties Union
Harrisburg Office
P. O. Box 11761
Harrisburg, PA 17108
(Phone) 717-238-2258
Email: infohbg@aclupa.org
Through advocacy, education and litigation, our attorneys, advocates, and volunteers work to preserve and promote civil liberties including the freedom of speech, the right to privacy, reproductive freedom of speech, and equal treatment under the law. We stand in defense of the rights of women and minorities, workers, students, immigrants, gay, lesbian, bisexual and transgender people and others who have seen bias and bigotry threaten the rights afforded to all of us in this country by the Constitution and the Bill of Rights.

Forensic Clemency and Parole Services
74 Garilee Lane
Elizabethtown, PA 17022
Forensic Clemency and Parole Services. They can assist you in preparing petitions for filing by collecting needed information.

Juvenile Lifers
P. O. Box 8077
Pittsburgh, PA 15216
Website: www.juvenilelifers.org
This is a not-for-profit organization dedicated to juveniles in the State of Pennsylvania and across the country who are serving sentences of life without parole.

Lewisburg Prison Project
P. O. Box 128
Lewisburg, PA 17837-0128
Email: info@lewisburgprisonproject.org

Mid Penn Legal Services
211 E. Locust Street
Clearfield, PA 16830
(Phone) 814-765-9646

Mid Penn Legal Services
3500 E. College Avenue
State College, PA 16801
(Phone) 814-238-4958

Neighborhood Legal Services Association

928 Penn Avenue
Pittsburgh, PA 15222-3799
(Phone) 412-255-6700
Website: https://nlsa.us

Northwest Legal Services

1001 State Street, Ste. 1200
Erie, PA 16501
(Phone) 814-452-6957

PRO BONO OFFICES IN PHILADELPHIA, PA

AIDS Law Project of Pennsylvania

1211 Chestnut Street, Ste. 600
Philadelphia, PA 19107
https://www.aidslawpa.org/on-line-intake

American Civil Liberties Union (ACLU)

(Philadelphia Office)
P.O. Box 40008
Philadelphia, PA 19106
(Phone) 215-592-1513
Email: info@aclupa.org

Community Legal Services

3638 North Broad Street
Philadelphia, PA 19140
(Phone) 215-227-2400

Community Legal Services of Philadelphia

1424 Chestnut Street
Philadelphia, PA 19102
(Phone) 215-981-3700

Congresso de Latinos Unidos

216 West Somerset Street
Philadelphia, PA 19133

Defender Association of Philadelphia
437 Chestnut Street, Ste. 501
Philadelphia, PA 19106
(Phone) 215-928-0520

Defender Association of Philadelphia, Cap Defender
121 North Broad Street
Philadelphia, PA 19106
(Phone) 215-557-4961

Equality Advocates Pennsylvania
1211 Chestnut Street
Philadelphia, PA 19107

HIAS and Council Migration Service of Philadelphia
2100 Arch Street, 3rd Floor
Philadelphia, PA 19103

Homeless Advocacy Project
1429 Walnut Street
Philadelphia, PA 19102

Human Rights Coalition
4123 Lancaster Avenue
Philadelphia, PA 19104

Legal Clinic for the Disabled
1513 Race Street
Philadelphia, PA 19102

Pennsylvania Client Assistance Program
(CAP)
1617 JFK Boulevard
Philadelphia, PA 19103

Pennsylvania Institutional Law Project
The Cast Iron Building
718 Arch Street, Suite 304 South
Philadelphia, PA 19106
Phone: 215.925.2966
Email: info@pilp.org

Penn Law Civil Practice Clinic
3501 Sansom Street
Philadelphia, PA 19104

Penn Law Transnational Clinic
Attn: Robert Dunham
3400 Chestnut Street
Philadelphia, PA 19104
(Phone) 215-451-6500

Pennsylvania Post-Conviction Defender Organization
Attn: Robert Dunham
The Lafayette Building, Ste. 501
437 Chestnut Street
Philadelphia, PA 19106-2414
(Phone) 215-451-6500

Philadelphia Volunteers for the Indigent Program (VIP)
1500 Walnut Street
Philadelphia, PA 19102

Philly VIP
42 South 15th Street, 4th Floor
Philadelphia, PA
(Phone) 215-523-9550
Website: www.phillyvip.org

Public Interest Law Center of Philadelphia
1500 JFK Blvd., Ste. 802
Philadelphia, PA 19102
Website: www.https://pubintlaw.org/

Senior Law Center
1500 JFK Boulevard, Ste. 151
Philadelphia, PA 19102

Services to Elder Prisoners, Pennsylvania Prison Society
245 North Broad Street, Ste. 300
Philadelphia, PA 19107

Temple Legal Aid Office
1719 N. Broad Street
Philadelphia, PA 19122

The Elderly Law Project, Temple University
1719 N. Broad Street
Philadelphia, PA 19122

The Public Interest Law Center of Philadelphia
125 S. 9th Street
Philadelphia, PA 19107

Women Against Abuse Legal Center
100 South Broad Street, 5th Floor
Philadelphia, PA 19107
(Phone) 215-386-1280

Women in Transition
21 South 12th Street
Philadelphia, PA 19107
(Phone) 215-564-5301

Women's Law Project
(Main Office)
125 S. 9th Street, Suite 300
Philadelphia, PA 19107
(Phone) 215-928-9801
Website: www.womenslawproject.org

Women's Law Project
425 Sixth Avenue, Ste. 1860
Pittsburgh, PA 15219
(Phone) 412-227-0301
Email: infopitt@womenslawptoject.org

PRO BONO OFFICES IN PENNSYLVANIA

Allegheny County Lawyer Referral Service
(Phone) 412-261-5555
Website: www.paprobono.net
Website: www.probono.net – National Public Defender Forum

American Civil Liberties Union

(Harrisburg Office)
P.O. Box 11761
Harrisburg, PA 17108
(Phone) 717-238-2258
Email: infohbg@aclupa.org
Through advocacy, education, and litigation, our attorneys, advocates, and volunteer work to preserve and promote civil liberties including freedom of speech, the right to privacy, reproductive freedom of speech, and equal treatment under the law. We stand in defense of the rights of women and minorities, workers, students, immigrants, gay, lesbian, bisexual and transgender people and others who have seen bias and bigotry threaten the rights afforded to all of us in this country by the Constitution and the Bill of Rights.

American Civil Liberties Union

(Pittsburg Office)
313 Atwood Street
Pittsburgh, PA 15213
(Phone) 412-681-7736
Email: info@aclupgh.org
Website: www.aclupgh.org

Forensic Clemency and Parole Services

74 Garilee Lane
Elizabethtown, PA 17022
Forensic Clemency and Parole Services. They can assist you in preparing petitions for filing by collecting needed information.

Juvenile Lifers

P.O. Box 8077
Pittsburgh, PA 15216
Website: www.juvenilelifers.org
This is a not-for-profit organization dedicated to juveniles in the State of Pennsylvania and across the country who are serving sentences of life without parole.

Lackawanna Pro Bono

321 Spruce Street
Scranton, PA 18503
(Phone) 570-961-2715

Lewisburg Prison Project

P.O. Box 128
Lewisburg, PA 17837-0128
(Phone) 570-523-1104
Website: info@lewisburgprisonproject.org

Mid Penn Legal Services

211 E. Locust Street
Clearfield, PA 16830
(Phone) 814-765-9646

Mid Penn Legal Services

3500 E. College Avenue
State College, PA 16801
(Phone) 814-238-4958

Neighborhood Legal Services Association

928 Penn Avenue
Pittsburgh, PA 15222-3799
(Phone) 412-255-6700
Website: www.nlsa.us

Northwest Legal Services

1001 State Street, Ste. 1200
Erie, PA 16501
(Phone) 814-452-6957
Email: roakley@nwls.org
Website: www.nwls.org
They offer a range of civil legal services in the areas of family, health education, and employment. Offers help with government benefits and housing in the counties of Cameron, Crawford, Erie, Elk, Forest,
McKean, Mercer, Potter, and Warren. They also offer advice in areas of landlord/tenant, debt collection, sheriff's sales, school suspensions, and come custody advice.

Pennsylvania Bar Association

100 South Street
Harrisburg, PA 17108
(Phone) 800-932-0311
Email: info@pabar.org
Website: www.pabar.org

Pennsylvania Institutional Law Project

The Cast Iron Building
718 Arch Street, Ste. 304 South
Philadelphia, PA 19106
(Phone) 215-925-2966
Email: info@pilp.org

Pennsylvania Institutional Law Project

115 Farley Circle, Ste. 110
Lewisburg, PA 17837
(Phone) 570-661-9043
Email: info@pilp.org

PA Institutional Law Project

247 Fort Pitt Boulevard, 4th Floor
Pittsburgh, PA 15222
(Phone) 412-434-6004
Email: info@pilp.org

PA Institutional Law Project

247 Fort Pitt Blvd, 4th Floor
Pittsburgh, PA 15222
(Phone) 412-434-6004
Email: info@pilp.org

Pennsylvania Legal Services

118 Locust Street
Harrisburg, PA 17101-1414
(Phone) 717-236-9486
Website: www.palegalservices.org

Pittsburgh Legal Service Directory by Pro Bono Pittsburgh

Website: www.nlsa.us/resources/linke/informationresources/legal_services_directory.pdf

Pittsburgh Pro Bono Partnership

Koppers Building
Pittsburgh, PA 15219
(Phone) 412-402-6641
Pro Bono Center Phone: 412-402-6677
Website: www.acbf.org/Attorney_Services/Pittsburgh_Pro_Bono.asp

Women's Law Project

(Pittsburgh Office)
425 Sixth Avenue, Ste. 1860
Pittsburgh, PA 15219
(Phone) 412-227-0301
E-mail: infopitt@womenslawproject.org

Women's Law Project

(Pittsburgh Office)
1705 Allegheny Building
Pittsburgh, PA 15219
(Phone) 412-232-0276

RHODE ISLAND

ACLU of Rhode Island

128 Dorrance Street, Ste. 220
Providence, RI 02903
(Phone) 401-831-7171
Email: riaclu.org
Website: www.riaclu.org
Provides limited assistance to prisoners. Services are restricted to post-conviction, habeas corpus, prison conditions, and direct referrals. Especially concerned with prison problems that raise significant First Amendment or due process issued.

Rhode Island Bar Association Volunteer Lawyer Program

115 Cedar Street
Providence, RI 02903-1082
(Phone) 401-421-7799

Rhode Island Legal Services

56 Pine Street, 4th Floor
Providence, RI 02903
(Phone) 401-274-2652

Volunteer Lawyer Program

Chamber of Commerce
41 Sharpe Drive
Cranston, RI
(Phone) 401-421-7558

SOUTH CAROLINA

ACLU of South Carolina
2712 Middleburg Drive, Ste. 104
Columbia, SC 29204
(Phone) 803-799-5151
Email: intake@aclusc.org
Website: www.aclusc.org
Provides limited assistance to prisoners. Services are restricted to post-incarceration, habeas corpus, prison conditions, and direct referrals.

Alston Wilkes Society
3519 Medical Drive
Columbia, SC 29203
(Phone) 803-799-2490
Email: glockhart@alstonwilkessociety.org
Website: www.alstonwilkessociety.org
Statewide social service organization that provides a broad range of direct services and referral assistance to offenders, ex-offenders, and their immediate families. Provides assistance to prisoners regarding parole and release planning, as well as advocacy and legislative services. Operates halfway houses for adult offenders, group homes for emotionally disturbed juveniles, and a facility for homeless male veterans. Provides public information and educational programs to citizens of South Carolina and provides a range of volunteer services to adults and juveniles.

Another Chance 4 Legal, LLC
P.O. Box 78
Mullins, SC 29574
(Phone) 843-879-8361
Email: anotherchance4legal@gmail.com

Federal Death Penalty Resource Center
Attn: David I. Bruck
P.O. Box 11744
Columbia, SC 803-763-1044

Habeas Assistance & Training Project
Attn: John H. Blume
P. O. Box 11744
Columbia, SC 29211
(Phone) 803-765-1044

Lowcountry Legal Aid, Inc.
167-A Bluffton Road
Bluffton, SC 29910
(Phone) 843-815-1570

Palmetto Innocence Project
P.O. Box 11623
Columbia, SC 29211
(Phone) 803-779-0005

South Carolina Legal Services
2803 Carner Avenue
Charleston, SC 29405
(Phone) 843-720-7044

South Carolina Legal Services
69 Robert Smalls Parkway, Ste. 3-A
Beaufort, SC 29902
(Phone) 843-521-0623

South Carolina Legal Services
2109 Bull Street
PO Box 7187
Columbia, SC 29201-7187
(Phone) 888-346-5592

South Carolina Post-Conviction Defender Organization
P. O. Box 11311
Columbia, SC 29201

South Carolina Post-Conviction Defender Organization
1247 Sumter Street, Ste. 303
Columbus, SC 29201
(Phone) 803-765-0651

SOUTH DAKOTA

ACLU of the Dakotas
Manchester Building
112 N. University Drive, Suite 301
Fargo, ND 58102-4661
(Phone) 701-461-7290
Email: dakaclu.com

East River Legal Services

335 N. Main Avenue, Ste. 300
Sioux Falls, SD 57102
(Phone) 605-336-9230

Second Judicial Circuit Pro Bono Project

335 N. Main Avenue
Sioux Falls, SD 57104
(Phone) 605-336-9230

State Bar of South Dakota

Access to Justice
222 E. Capitol Avenue
Pierre, SD 57501.
(Phone) 1-855-287-3510

TENNESSEE

ACLU of Tennessee

P. O. Box 120160
Nashville, TN 37212
(Phone) 615-320-7142
Website: www.aclu.tn.org
Handles habeas corpu s, if a civil rights question is involved, and prison and jail conditions cases.
Provides direct referrals and legal assistance regarding discrimination based on AIDS/HIV.

Tennessee Association of Legal Services

211 Union Street, Ste. 833
Nashville, TN 37102-1536
(Phone) 615-242-0438

Tennessee Coalition to Abolish State Killing

Boox 120552
Nashville, TN 37212
(Phone) 615-256-3906
Email: tcask@tcask.org
Website: www.tcask.org
Coordinates legislative and community opposition to the death penalty. Publishes quarterly
newsletter, *Tennessee Lifelines,* free to Tennessee death-row prisoners,

Tennessee Post-Conviction Defender

Attn: Donald Dawson
1320 Andrew Jackson Building
500 Deadrick Street
Nashville, TN 37243
(Phone) 615-741-9331

TEXAS

ACLU of Texas

P.O. Box 8306
Houston, TX 77288
(Phone) 713-942-8146
Website: www.aclutx.org

ACLU of Texas Prison and Jail Accountability Project

P.O. Box 12905
Austin, TX 78711-2905
(Phone) 512-478-7309
Email: info@aclutx.org
Website: www.aclutx.org
Handles city, county, state, and federal prison condition cases.

Ashley Burleson, Esquire

Attorney and Counselor at Law
1001 Texas Avenue., Ste. 1400
Houston, TX 77002
Post-conviction state and federal habeas corpus, parole representation, and family law for Texas inmates

Disability Rights Texas

2222 West Braker Lane
Austin, TX 78758
(Phone) 512-454-4816

Fulbright & Jaworski, LLP

1301 McKinny, Ste. 5100
Houston, TX 77010-3095
(Phone) 713-651-5151
Stewart W. Gagnon, Chair of Pro Bono Committee
Email: sgagnon@fulbright.com

Harvey Cox, Esquire

P.O. Box 1551
Weatherford, TX 76086
(Phone) 817-596-8457
Website: www.prisonconsultant.com
Specializes in helping state inmates with transfers, grievances, and parole.

Innocence Project of Texas

1511 Texas Avenue
Lubbock, TX 79401
(Phone) 806-744-6525
Website: www.ipoftexas.org

Jackson & Reed Law Firm

601 Sawyer, Ste. 105
Houston, TX 77007
(Phone) 713-429-1405
Affordable attorneys that offer experience and compassionate defense, parole, and post-conviction work.

Law Office of William Savoie

909 Texas Avenue, Ste. 205
Houston, TX 77002
(Phone) 832-341-4802
Email: wlsavoielaw@gmail.com
Parole, post-conviction, pardons, prison planning (power of attorney, probate/trust for families)

Texas Civil Rights Project

1405 Montopolis Drive
Austin, TX 78741-3438
(Phone) 512-474-5073
Email: tcrp.questions@gmail.com

Texas CURE

4121 Burning Tree Lane
Garland, TX 75042
(Phone) 972-276-9865
Email: dill.c@tx.rr.com
Website: www.txcure.org

Texas Innocence Network
University of Houston Law Center
100 Law Center
Houston, TX 77204

Texas Legal Services Center
815 Brazos, Ste. 1100
Austin, TX 78701
(Phone) 512-477-6000

Texas Defender Service
Attn: Mandy Welch
412 Main Street, Ste. 700
Houston, TX 77266
(Phone) 713-222-7788

Texas Resource Center
Attn: Eden Harrington
205 West 9th Street, Ste. 201
Austin, TX 78767-0280
(Phone) 512-320-8300

Thurgood Marshall School of Law Innocence Project
3100 Cleburne Street
Houston, TX 77004
(Phone) 713-313-1139

University of Texas Center for Actual Innocence
University of Texas School of Law
727 East Dean Keeton Street
Austin, TX 78705

Walter Reaves, Esquire
100 N. 6th Street, Ste. 902
Waco, TX 76701
(Phone) 254-781-3588
Website: www.waco-criminal-attorney.com
Criminal defense attorney Walter Reaves has been practicing law in Waco, Texas, for 37 years. In addition to his membership in the State Bar of Texas, Mr. Reaves is also a member of the Texas Criminal Defense Lawyers Association. His office offers work on post-conviction, appeals, case

evaluation and motions, criminal defense, expungements and disclosures. His website offers 10 FREE e-books! Titles include "Don't Hire the Wrong Lawyer," "Hiring a Criminal Lawyer," "You've Been Arrested; What Do You Do Now," "Freedom Through Science," "An Inmate's Guide to Habeas Corpus," and others. Have your family download them, print them out, and mail them to you.

Wesleyan Innocence Project
1515 Commerce Street
Fort Worth, TX 76102

UTAH

ACLU of Utah
355 North 300 W, #1
Salt Lake City, UT 84103
(Phone) 801-521-9289
Email: aclu@acluutah.org
Website: www.acluutah.org
Reviews complaints resulting in systemic violations or prisoner rights. Monthly meetings with prison officials to resolve ongoing problems; medical care, mental health, and general conditions

Prisoner Information Network
(PIN)
P. O. Box 16517
Salt Lake City, UT 84116
(Phone) 801-355-0234
Email: pin@prisonernetwork.com
A resource for prisoners and their families in Utah. Provides hygiene kits to prisoners being released in Utah. Holds monthly outreach meetings and publishes newsletter, "Behind the Wire." Also publishes the *Utah Prisoner Resource Guide,* $4.00 for prisoners and $10.00 for people in the free world.

Rocky Mountain Innocence Center
358 South 700 East, B235
Salt Lake City, UT 84102
(Phone) 801-355-1888
Website: www.rminnocence.org

Utah Legal Services
205 N. 400 W
Salt Lake City, UT 84103
(Phone) 801-328-8891

Utah Legal Services

455 N. University Avenue, Ste. 100
Provo, UT 84601
Website: www.utahlegalservices.org
(Phone) 801-374-6766

Utah Legal Services, Inc.

254 West 4th Street, 2nd Floor
Salt Lake City, UT 84101
(Phone) 801-328-8891

VERMONT

ACLU of Vermont

137 Elm Street
Montpelier, VT 05602
(Phone) 802-223-6304
Email: unfo@acluvt.org
Website: www.acluvt.org

Prisoners' Rights Office

6 Baldwin Street, 4th Floor
Montpelier, VT 05633
(Phone) 802-828-3194

Vermont Catholic Organization

(Phone) 802-658-6110 x312
Email: charities@vermontcatholic.org
Provides one-on-one pastoral counseling, family visitation, prisoner-supervised passes, and referral services. Services are limited to Vermont offenders, ex-offenders, and their families. Also provides Catholic Mass and other church services. Ensures that each prisoner receives a Christmas gift – i.e., socks, shampoo, writing paper, etc. Furnishes clothing whenever possible to needy prisoners. Assists ex-offenders with employment and housing assistance.

Vermont Legal Aid

177 Western Avenue, Ste 1
St. Johnsbury, VT 05819
(Phone) 802-748-8721

Vermont Legal Aid

56 College Street
Montpelier, VT 05602
(Phone) 802-223-6377
 800-889-2047

Vermont Legal Aid

12 North Street
PO Box 1367
Burlington, VT 05401
(Phone) 802-863-5620

Vermont's Pro Bono Program

274 North Winooski Avenue
Burlington, VT 05401-3621
(Phone) 802-863-7153

VIRGINIA

AIDS/HIV Services Group

P. O. Box 2322
Charlottsville, VA 22902
(Phone) 434-979-7714
Email: info@aidsservices.org
Website: www.aidsservices.org
Offers services to individuals with HIV/AIDS who are in the local jail, including emotional support, informational support, information packets, and assistance with post-release planning – housing, employment, etc. Also offers supportive services to family members and friends of individuals with HIV/AIDS who are incarcerated.

ACLU of Virginia

530 East Main Street, Suite 310
Richmond, VA 23219
(Phone) 804-644-8022
Email: intake@acluva.org
Website: www.acluva.org
Handles select litigation limited to state prison facilities and county jails.

Institute for Criminal Justice Healthcare

1700 Diagonal Road, Ste. 110
Alexandria, VA 22314
(Phone) 703-836-0024

Offender Aid and Restoration of Arlington County

1400 N. Uhle Street, Ste. 704
Arlington, VA 22201
(Phone) 703-228-7030
Email: info@oaronline.org
Website: www.oaronline.org
Provides support, emergency assistance, identification, direct referrals, and planning for transition into the community. Prepares clients to obtain and maintain suitable employment. *Limited* to residents of Arlington County, City of Alexandria, and City of Falls Church.

Offender Aid and Restoration of Charlottesville/Albemarle

Attn: Patricia Smith
750 Harris Street, Ste. 207
Charlottesville, VA 22903
(Phone) 434-296-2441
Email: cdodds@oar-jacc.org

Pro Bono Opportunities in the Virginia Bar Association

1111 E. Main Street, Ste. 905
Richmond, VA 23219
(Phone) 804-644-0041
Website: www.thevba@vba.org

Virginia Post-Conviction Assistance Project

P. O. Box 506
Richmond, VA 23204-0506
(Phone) 804-643-6845

Virginia Poverty Law Center

201 West Broad Street, Ste. 302
Richmond, VA 23220
(Phone) 804-782-9430

WASHINGTON

ACLU of Washington

901 5th Avenue, Ste. 630
Seattle, WA 98164

Evergreen Legal Services

101 Yesler Way, Ste. 300
Seattle, WA 98104
(Phone) 205-464-5933

Freedom Documents, LLC

P. O. Box 4093
Spanaway, WA 98387
(Phone) 253-344-0990
Website: www.freedomdocumentsllc.com
They specialize in clemency and parole packets but can be a go-to for any other typing
and preparation of documents. 30 years within the Criminal Justice System, experience at all levels.

Innocence Project NW Clinic

University of Washington School of Law
William H. Gates Hall, Ste. 265
P.O. Box 85110
Seattle, WA 98145

NW Immigrant Rights Project

Eastern Washington Office
212 Sunnyside Avenue, Ste. 270
Granger, WA 98932
Website: www.nwirp.org
They promote justice for low-income immigrants by pursuing and defending their legal status. They
also focus on direct legal services, supported by education and public policy work.

Spokane County Public Defender

Attn: John Rodgers
1033 W. Gardner
Spokane, WA 99260
(Phone) 509-477-4246
By court appointment only. Handles adult felony, juvenile felony, misdemeanor and county
misdemeanor crimes. Also handles civil commitments and juvenile dependency cases.

Timothy C. Chiang-Lin, PLLC

2155 112th Avenue NE
Bellevue, WA 98004
Website: www.chiang-lin.com
This law office represents all individuals who suffer from childhood sex abuse in Washington and
Oregon

Western Washington Office
615 2ND Avenue, Ste. 400
Seattle, WA 98104
(Phone) 206-587-4009

WASHINGTON, DC

ACLU of the National Capital Area
Legal Department or
Fritz Mulhauser
1400 20th Street NW, Ste. 119
Washington, DC 20036-5920
(Phone) 202-457-0800
Website: www.aclu-nca.org

ACLU NPP
ACLU National Prison Project
915 15th Street NW, 7th Floor
Washington, DC 20005

American Bar Association
Death Penalty Representation Project
Contact: Elisabeth Semel
740 15th Street NW, Ste. 1060
Washington, DC 20005-1009
(Phone) 202-662-1995
Email: esemel@aol.com
Website: www.abanet.org/

Christian Legal Aid of DC
907 Maryland Avenue NE
Washington, DC 20002
(Phone) 202-710-0592

DC Prisoner's Project
Washington Lawyer's Committee for Civil Rights and Urban Affairs
11 Dupont Circle NW, Suite 400
Washington, DC 20036
Advocates for humane treatment and dignity of people charged under Washington, DC, law – even if you're being held anywhere in the federal system. They focus on health and medical issues, abuse, religious rights, mental health, hearing impaired issues, and some parole matters. Letters should provide as much detail and chronology of the situation as possible.

Domestic Violence Intake

500 Indiana Avenue NW, Room 4235
Washinton, DC 20001
(Phone) 202-879-0152

Fried, Frank, Harris Shriver & Jacobson

1001 Pennsylvania Avenue NW
Washington, DC 20004
(Phone) 202-639-7000
Contact: Karen T. Grisez, Public Service & Pro Bono Counsel

Legal Aid, DC

1331 H Street NW, Ste. 350
Washington, DC 20005
(Phone) 202-628-1161

Legal Information Help Line

Washington, DC
(Phone) 202-626-3499

Mid-Atlantic Innocence Project

4801 Massachusetts Avenue NW
Washington, DC 20016
(Phone) 202-274-4404
Email: VanBuskirkC.MAIP@GMAIL.COM
Website: www.exonerate
The Mid-Atlantic Innocence Project (MAIP) is a nonprofit organization dedicated to correcting and preventing the conviction of innocent people in the District of Columbia, Maryland, and Virginia. Through our Board of Directors, a staff of one full-time and one part-time lawyer, a project assistant and attorney and student volunteers, we identify innocent prisoners in our region. We then provide them with pro bono investigative and legal assistance so they can obtain their freedom.

National Association of Criminal Defense Attorneys

Attn: Paul Petterson
1627 K Street NW, Ste. 1200
Washington, DC 20006
(Phone) 202-872-8688, ext. 224

National CURE

P. O. Box 2310
Washington, DC 20013
(Phone) 202-789-2126
Email: cure@curenational.org
Website: www.curenational.org

Prisoners' Rights Program

Attn: Ryan Roberts
633 Indiana Avenue NW
Washington, DC 20004
(Phone) 202-628-1200
Services limited to prisoners confined in DC correctional facilities. Provides legal advice and assistance with conditions of confinement issues generally, including living conditions, access to adequate medical, dental, and psychiatric care, access to the courts, confinement to special housing units, visitation issues, and the right to practice one's religion. No criminal matters, motions to reduce sentence or detainers. Distribute free information memos on various prison law topics upon written request only

Project for Older Prisoners

2000 H Street NW
Washington, DC 20052
(Phone) 202-994-7001
Through George Washington University Law School, law students interview and evaluate older and geriatric inmates in obtaining parole or other forms of release from incarceration. Operates in six states: LA, MD, MI, NC, VA, and **DC**

The Veterans Consortium Pro Bono Program

2101 L Street NW, Suite 840
Washington, DC 20037
(Phone) 888-838-7727

WEST VIRGINIA

ACLU of West Virginia

P. O. Box 3952
Charleston, WV
(Phone) 304-345-9246
Email: mail@acluwv.org
Website: www.acluwv.org

Legal Aid of West Virginia

1025 Main Street
Wheeling, WV 26003
(Phone) 304-232-1260
Website: www.legalaidwv.org

Legal Aid of West Virginia

115 S. Kanawha Street
Beckley, WV 25801
(Phone) 304-255-0561
Website: www.legalaidwv.org

West Virginia Innocence Project

P.O. Box 6130
Morgantown, WV 26506
(Phone) 304-293-7249

West Virginia Legal Service Plan

1003 Quarrier Street, Ste. 700
Charleston, WV 25301
(Phone) 304-342-6814

WISCONSIN

ACLU of Wisconsin

207 East Buffalo Street, Ste. 325
Milwaukee, WI 53202
(Phone) 414-272-4032 x16
Email: inquiries@aclu-wi.org
Website: www.aclu-wi.org

Law Office of Matthew S. Pinix

1200 East Capital Drive., Ste. 360
Milwaukee, WI 53211
(Phone) 414-963-6164
Website: www.pinixlawoffice.com
Specializes in criminal appeal cases and civil rights. They handle direct appeal, post-conviction, and habeas cases in the States of Wisconsin and Illinois only.

Legal Action of Wisconsin

230 West Wells Street, Room 800
Milwaukee, WI 53202
(Phone) 414-278-7777

Wisconsin Innocence Project
University of Wisconsin, Madison
Attn: Lindsey Smith
975 Bascom Mall
Madison, WI 53706-1399

WYOMING

Legal Services for Southeast Wyoming
1620 Central Avenue, Ste. 200
Cheyenne, WY 82001-4575
(Phone) 307-634-1566

OFFICE OF VOCATIONAL REHABILITATION

Website: www.dli.pa.gov/ovr
The Office of Vocational Rehabilitation (OVR) serves people who have disabilities that present a substantial impediment to employment. Services are provided to individuals, including those who are returning to society from prison, to prepare for, secure, retain, advance in or regain employment.

Harrisburg Office
Forum Place
655 Walnut Street, 8th Floor
Harrisburg, PA 17101
(Phone) 717-787-7634

Philadelphia Office
801 Market Street, Ste. 6043
Philadelphia, PA 19107
(Phone) 215-560-1900

Pittsburgh Office
531 Penn Avenue
Pittsburgh, PA 15222
(Phone) 412-392-4950

Reading Office
3602 Kutztown Road, Ste. 200
Reading, PA 19605
(Phone) 610-621-5800

Wilkes-Barre Office
8 West Market Street, Ste. 200
Wilkes-Barre, PA 18701
(Phone) 570-826-2011

STATE RE-ENTRY FACILITIES

G.R.O.W.N.
8410 Bustleton Avenue, Ste. 2
Philadelphia, PA 19152
(Phone) 267-694-1003
Website: www.wearegrown.org

Pennsylvania Prison Society
245 N. Broad Street, Ste. 300
Philadelphia, PA 19107-1518
(Phone) 215-564-6005
Website: www.prisonsociety.org
Email: customerservice@prisonsociety.org

CHAPTER 3

3. NATIONAL PRO BONO AND LEGAL AID PROGRAM DIRECTORY

ACLU National Prison Project
915 15TH Street NW, Ste. 620
Washington, DC 20005
(Phone) 202-893-4930

American Bar Association
321 North Clark Street
Chicago, IL 60610
(Phone) 800-285-2221
Website: www.findlegalhelp.org
Their website is one of the best available. It allows you to search for a list of legal resources available in your area, including pro bono or inexpensive lawyers, help in dealing with lawyers, legal information, self-help materials, and more.

Bluhm Legal Clinic
357 E Chicago Avenue
Chicago, IL 60611
(Phone) 312-503-8576
The Center on Wrongful Convictions (CWC) will consider cases of actual innocence, meaning that you must be in no way responsible for the crime for which you were convicted.

Centurion
1000 Herrontown Road
Princeton, NJ 08540
Centurion is a national non-profit organization that is dedicated to the vindication of the wrongly convicted. They take on the hard cases, the ones others leave behind. They re-investigate the crime, uncovering lost evidence, finding new evidence, convincing a coerced witness to come forward with the truth, overturning false confessions, and sometimes even finding the real criminal. Centurion is an investigative organization that considers claims of factual innocence in rape and murder cases where an individual is serving more than 15 years before they will be eligible for parole or has been sentenced to death. They do not take on accidental death, self-defense cases, or cases where the defendant had any involvement whatsoever in the crime for which he/she was convicted.

Justice Denied

Justicedenied.org

The Justice Institute -- (Justice Denied is a trade name of The Justice Institute)

Email comments, suggestions, questions, etc. to: contact@justicedenied.org

Online catalog of attorneys who take on pro bono cases.

Law Help

Website: www.lawhelp.org/find-help

Law Help is an online resource that helps low and moderate-income people find free legal aid programs in their communities, answers to questions about their legal rights, court information, links to social service agencies, and more.

MNN, Inc.

Shani Burton, Esquire

244 5th Avenue, Ste. B-230

New York, NY 10001

NAACP National Prison Project

4805 Mt. Hope Drive

Baltimore, MD 21215

Website: www.naacp.org/programs/prison

National Center on Institutions & Alternatives (NCIA)

7222 Ambassador Road

Baltimore, MD 21244

(Phone) 410-265-1490

Website: www.ncianet.org

Email: aboring@ncianet.org

Contact: Alice Boring

Provides criminal justice services to defense attorneys, defendants, inmates, and court systems throughout the country.

National Center for Lesbian Rights

870 Market Street, Ste. 370

San Francisco, CA 94102

(Phone) 415-392-6257

Provides legal referrals for LGBTQ

National Center for Youth Law
405 14th Street, 15th Floor
Oakland, CA 94612
Provides information, referrals, technical assistance, or written materials; serves as co-counsel in cases affecting a large number of children and families; assists lawyers who are directly representing at-risk or incarcerated youth.

National Clemency Project, Inc.
3907 N. Federal Highway, Ste. 151
Pompano Beach, FL 33604
(Phone) 954-271-2304
Founded in 1988, they handle petitions for clemency and commutations in all 50 states.

National Clemency Project
8624 Camp Columbus Road
Hixon, TN 37343
35 years of clemency, parole assistance, and transfers under the International Prison Treaty

National Criminal Justice References Services
P.O. Box 6000
Rockville, MD 20849-6000
(Phone) 800-851-3420
Website: www.ncjrs.org

National Federal Legal Services
2392 N. Decatur Road
Decatur, GA 30033
Website: www.federalappealslawyer.com

- Federal Appellate Representation for all circuits and supreme court
  - Member of all federal circuits and supreme court
  - Over 150 appeals filed

- Federal 2255 Habeas Petitions anywhere in the United States
  - Representations
  - Pro Se Litigation, assistance, or representation
  - Over 200 Habeas represented

Experienced attorneys make the difference winning cases throughout the United States for over 20 years.

National Innocence Network

Website: www.innocencenetwork.org

This organization responds to claims of innocence and assists prisoners in locating appropriate help. If your case is accepted by a member of the National Innocence Network, they will offer support services.

National Innocence Project

40 Worth Street, Ste. 701
New York, NY 10013
Website: www.innocenceproject.org

Only handles cases where post-conviction DNA testing of evidence can yield conclusive evidence of innocence. Currently not accepting new cases from California, Ohio, Washington, or Wisconsin. See individual innocence projects for those states.

National Lawyers Guild

132 Nassau Street, Ste. 922
New York, NY 10038
(Phone) 212-679-5100
Website: www.nlgny.nlg.org

National Legal Aid and Defender Association

1140 Connecticut Avenue NW, Ste. 900
Washington, DC 20036
Website: www.nlada.org

National Post-Conviction Project

5348 Vegas Drive, Ste. 99
Las Vegas, NV 89108
(Phone) 702-969-7262
Email: admin@postconviction.org

The NPCP has over 60+ attorneys licensed throughout the United States, the Federal courts, and the United States Supreme Court

Pine Tree Legal Assistance

Website: www.ptla.org/probono.htm

Provides a list of organizations that provide referrals to lawyers who may be able to provide legal services for no cost or substantially reduced fees.

Pro Bono Institute

1025 Connecticut Avenue NW, Ste. 205
Washington, DC 20036
(Phone) 202-729-6699
Email: www.probonoinst.org

Pro Bono Services

151 West 30th Street, 6th Floor
New York, NY 10001
(Phone) 212-760-2554
Website: www.probono.net
Probono.net works to increase access to justice for low-income people by connecting attorneys to those most in need and provide legal tools to help individuals advocate for themselves.

Re-Sentencing Project

Center for Policy Research
2020 Pennsylvania Avenue NW, Ste. 465
Washington, DC 20006
They offer sentence reductions for assistance to federal agencies concerned with prison gang violence, homicide, drug trafficking, extortion, terrorism, and child exploitation. Prison advocacy through re-sentencing. Write for application and more information. (Please allow 6-8 weeks for a response.)

Special Litigation Section

US Department of Justice Civil Rights Division
950 Pennsylvania Avenue NE
Washington, DC 20530
Website: www.usdoj.gov/crt/split

The Innocence Network

Website: www.innocencenetwork.org
The Innocence Network is an affiliation of organizations from all over the world dedicated to providing pro bono legal and investigative services to individuals seeking to prove innocence of a crime for which they have been convicted.

United Consulting Services

11820 Old Drovers Way
Rockville, MD 20852
(Phone) 202-417-1239
We are certified legal specialists in ALL 50 states. We understand being incarcerated is stressful. However, you may have options. Let us find those options. We assist in the following: reduction/modification, transfers, parole issues, restoration of visits, wrongfully convicted, Second Chance Act, and more. Write us for our brochure!

Women's Prison Association

110 Second Avenue
New York, NY 10003
(Phone) 646-292-7740
Website: info@wpaonline.org

Police Transparency Project

The Need for Transparency

Without transparency, there can be no trust between the community and the police. Practices inside the Homicide Unit are largely hidden from the public. While some evidence of detective misconduct has been, and currently is, the subject of Internal Affairs investigations, those investigations cannot be generally accessed by defendants and/or their counsel, much less the general public. Moreover, after a defendant is convicted, he/she no longer has a "right" to discovery and cannot subpoena these records absent court approval.

Our Mission

The Police Transparency Project's mission is to compile documentation on police and prosecutorial misconduct and make it publicly accessible. The PTP collects data on unconstitutional interrogation patterns and practices used by Homicide detectives over the last three decades, which has resulted in countless wrongful convictions of actually innocent defendants. The Police Transparency Project seeks to gather information and documentation about specific homicide detectives' and supervisors' participation in these abuses and to make that information readily accessible to attorneys, defendants, and the public. It is hoped that this will help promote lasting systemic changes and facilitate an environment of transparency and trust between the police and the community.

Our Goal

The database will be a critical resource for use in criminal trials, appeals, and civil actions. Evidence that detectives investigating a particular homicide case had a history of utilizing this unconstitutional pattern and practice could, under the right factual circumstances, be used during trial to impeach the detective's trial testimony and/or as a basis on appeal to grant relief to wrongly-convicted defendants.

In addition, information compiled on the database will provide the statistical basis to identify the need for police training, policy changes and legislative initiatives. It is hoped that information gleaned from this database will help promote lasting systemic changes and facilitate an environment where Philadelphians can trust the reliability and constitutionality of homicide convictions in their city.

Tower Place
1400 Spring Garden St., #911
Philadelphia, PA
Email: thimebaughesq@earthlink.net
        Tel: 484-686-3279

Director:
Teri B. Himebaugh, M.D., L.I.M.

Teri B. Himebaugh has a Juris Doctor and a Legal Master's degree. She is a sole practitioner and has been practicing law for more than 33 years. Teri has served as co-chair for the International Human

Right section of the Philadelphia Bar Association, as well as on the Board of the American Civil Liberties Union and is a current member of the US. District Court Prisoner Civil Rights Panel.

Managing Director:
Kathryn Himebaugh, MSW

Kathryn Himebaugh has a Master's Degree in Social Work Administration. She specializes in resource referral, re-entry services for exonerees, and community organizing.

Private Investigators
Richard Strohm
Jeff Stein

Legal Counsel
Sam Stretton, Esquire

CHAPTER 4

4. LAW SCHOOL LEGAL PROJECT DIRECTORY

American University – Washington College of Law
Mid-Atlantic Innocence Project
(District of Columbia, Maryland, and Virginia cases only)
2000 H Street NW
Washington, DC 20052
(Phone) 202-995-4586
Website: www.exonerate.org

Blackstone School of Law
P.O. Box 899
Emmaus, PA 18094-0899
(Phone) 610-967-3323

Chico State University
Penal Law Project
25 Main Street, Ste. 102
Chico, CA 95929
(Phone) 530-898-4354
Website: www.aschico.com/clic/programsandadvocacy

Georgetown University Law Center
Pro Bono Institute
1025 Connecticut Avenue NW, Suite 205
Washington, DC 20036
(Phone) 202-729-6699
Website: www.probonoinst.org

Hamline University School of Law
Innocence Project of Minnesota
1536 Hewitt Avenue
St. Paul, MN 55104
(Phone) 651-523-3152

Indiana University School of Law
Wrongful Conviction Clinic
530 W. New York Street, Room 111
Indianapolis, IN 46202-3225
(Phone) 317-274-5551

Rutgers University School of Law Constitutional Litigation Clinic

Innocence Project for Justice
123 Washington Street
Newark, NJ 07102

Santa Clara University

Northern California Innocence Project
500 El Camino Road
Santa Clara, CA 95053
(Phone) 408-554-4361
Email: lawadmissions@scu.edu

Seton Hall University School of Law

The Last Resort Innocence Project
One Newark Center
1109 Raymond Boulevard

Stanford Law School

Crown Quadrangle
559 Nathan Abbott Way
Stanford, CA 94305-8610
(Phone) 650-723-2465
Website: law.stanford.edu/organizations/programs-and-centers/Stanford-three-strikes-project
The Stanford Three Strikes Project is the only legal organization in the country devoted to addressing
excessive sentences imposed under California's Three Strikes sentencing law.

Temple University Beasley School of Law

Pennsylvania Innocence Project
1719 North Broad Street
Philadelphia, PA 19122
(Phone) 215-204-4255
Email: innocenceprojectpa@temple.edu

Thurgood Marshall School of Law

Innocence Project
3100 Cleburne Street
Houston, TX 77004
(Phone) 713-313-1139

UC Davis School of Law

Prison Law Clinic
One Shields Avenue, TB30
Davis, CA 95616
(Phone) 530-752-6942
Website: www.law.ucdavis.edu/faculty/Murphy

University of Houston Law Center

Texas Innocence Network
100 Law Center
Houston, TX 77204

University of Mississippi School of Law

Mississippi Innocence Project
P.O. Box 1848
University, MS 38677
(Phone) 662-915-5206

University of New Mexico School of Law

Innocence and Justice Project
1117 Stanford NE
Albuquerque, MM 87131-0001
(Phone) 505-277-2671

University of Texas School of Law

Center for Actual Innocence
727 Dean Keeton Street
Austin, TX 78705

University of Virginia School of Law

580 Massie Road
Charlottesville, VA 22903
(Phone) 434-924-7354
Email: probono@law.virginia.edu
Website: www.law.virginia.edu/publicserv/probono

University of Washington School of Law

Innocence Project NW Clinic
William H. Gates Hall, Ste. 265
P.O. Box 85110
Seattle, WA 98145
Website: www.law.washington.edu/ipnw

University of Wisconsin

Wisconsin Innocence Project
975 Bascom Mall
Madison, WI 53706-1399
All law students are required to do a minimum of 25 hours of pro bono work annually. In order for their hours to count, the work must be unpaid, law-related, and supervised by a licensed attorney or a law school faculty member.

West Virginia University College of Law

West Virginia Innocence Project
P.O. Box 6130
Morgantown, WV 26506
(Phone) 304-293-7249

William Mitchell College of Law

Legal Assistance to Minnesota Prisoners
875 Summit Avenue, Room 254
St. Paul, MN 55105
(Phone) 651-290-6413
Website: www.wmitchell.edu/legal-practice-center

INTRODUCTION

Now that you are out of prison and once again a citizen of society, that means you are no longer just another prison number inside the system. However, although you have a fresh start in life and the world is whatever you decide to make it, just because you left prison, have your identity back, and whatever bad you did is long in the past behind you, doesn't mean that everything you did just goes away like it never happened now that you're out. Unfortunately, that's not how the system or our society works, even though, technically, if the whole fundamental reasoning behind criminals being sentenced to a period of incarceration isn't for punishment but as a way for them to pay their "debt" to society and rehabilitate themselves, then I strongly believe that it should work exactly like that.

Where ex-offenders are given a complete fresh start upon being released and present having paid their "debt" to society in full, this would mean getting a clean slate coming back into society not even as an ex-offender but as a regular, law-abiding citizen who has no criminal or arrest record; all of their felonies expunged from their record automatically. So there is no immediate negative judgmental stigma against them or a red flag looming over their heads just because they have come from prison, but, no. That would be too much, like, right? And instead, the reality of your recent incarceration experience is a huge red flag to everyone in society.

And so one of your first big challenges will be for you to overcome that red flag by means that you may not be so receptive to do, especially having just come from being in prison for many years. And it's very likely you still have your prison mentality which, like any habit, takes time and effort to break away from. In order to restore your reputation and remove that big red flag from over top of your head, you must go above and beyond to prove to everyone that you're no longer that "bad" person that you once were, that now you're a responsible, trustworthy, and law-abiding member of society.

Yes. Admittedly, I agree that it sucks having no other choice except to do something that no one who is like us ever wants to do, but after all, this is the real challenge of re-entry: to find out just how serious we are about bettering ourselves and succeeding in our new life. Unfortunately, the truth is as serious as you might believe you are, and as hard as you try to make it out there, the odds are stacked against you. Statistically, 70 percent of ex-offenders within three years of their release don't make it out in the world, and they return back to prison. So I guess the real question you should ask yourself is, where will you be in the next three years? Will you be in the 30% who actually succeed and live happily ever after, if such a thing even exists, or will you fall in with the other 70% who may or may not have tried hard to better themselves and become successful but failed somewhere along the way and ended back in prison?

If right now you're thinking anything along the lines of, "screw all this bullshit that this wannabe self-help guru fake-ass James Patterson-writing inmate is talking about, I can succeed on my own terms without having to jump through hoops; I don't have to prove myself to anyone; who the fuck are they that I should even give a damn about what they think of me," then you're probably just as much of a stubborn asshole as I was when I got released from prison all three times. And we all know how each one of those journeys had ended for me. I never made it more than two years out on the street before I ended up back in prison, all due to the self-destructive, fuck-you mentality I had.

After years of dealing with incarceration, there are very few ex-offenders who actually re-enter society with an upbeat, positive, can-do attitude. I know that I never did. Despite how happy I was to be back on the streets, it took me a while to finally shake having the guarded, aggressive and negative mentality many prisoners adopt while they're incarcerated. More often than not, an ex-offender's re-entry is filled with anxiety and uncertainty, uncertain how people will receive them, how they will act towards them and think about them, uncertain about their relationships with their family, friends, and significant other, uncertain where they'll live, how they're going to make money, and uncertain whether or not they'll find a job, succeed on the outside or end up failing and becoming another recidivism statistic.

You know how they always say when you're playing sports that the game is 60% mental and only 40% strength and skills and that your attitude wins championships? Well, that's also especially true for ex-offenders who are transitioning back into society from prison. Changing your prison mentality to a game-winning attitude is going to be one of your first difficult challenges you will have to overcome as soon as you step outside of the prison gates. After all, you're coming from a locked-down, caged environment where you really have no control over your own life and from which you likely suffered from feeling worthless, rejected, hated, and unwanted. Having had such a negative attitude for years while incarcerated, ex-offenders often don't realize how bad their attitude really is, but to others such as their family, friends, parole officer and potential employers, it's painfully obvious.

Not surprisingly, those negative attitudes affect their overall outlook on re-entry and motivation to put the hard work in to succeed. Pace yourself. No one ever wanted to admit it, especially to themselves, but coming from an environment like prison, it takes time to adjust back to the way things work on the outside. Let's face it: While you were in prison, you didn't really have to make many life-changing, important, or difficult decisions. You had a strict daily schedule down to the minute. You knew exactly where you had to go, what you had to do, when you had to do it, and everything you needed was provided to you for free: laundry services, clothing, three hot meals a day, recreational activities, 60 channels of cable and new DVD movies played daily on your TV in your cell, tablets that you can buy music, video games, and email people on the outside, video visits, college and vocational and GED schooling, paying jobs, down to toilet paper and envelopes whenever you needed it. If this wasn't a book about ex-offender re-entry, that would sound like the perfect community to live in. Well, you can join that community for the low price of committing a felony and getting sentenced to live in such a "perfect little community" for the next several years.

I know how you are likely feeling now that you're finally out of prison and back on the streets, anxious and excited all at the same time, with a little fear and uneasiness probably mixed in as well. You spent countless nights in your cell thinking about all of the many things you want to do as soon as you get out. And now that day has arrived and you're finally getting released, all of a sudden, that list of things that you've dreamt of doing your first day home every night for the last however many years you've been down is now the only thing that's on your mind as you walk out of the prison gates.

As someone who has experienced that first day out three times now, let me give you some cautionary advice. Take a couple deep breaths, calm down, control the racing thoughts, and take your time doing everything, and don't rush. From now on, with parole, sobriety, and re-entry, you're walking a tight line, and every single decision you make has to be the right decision. No pressure, right? Now that you're free, you have all the time in the world to do everything on your first day out list of the things you want to accomplish. But just because I call it a first day out list doesn't mean that you should attempt and do everything all in your very first day home, although I'm certain that you'll probably be very tempted to try.

The truth is, you likely won't be able to complete everything for at least a little while, and maybe you accomplish a couple things on your list on your very first day, but all the rest likely will be accomplished over the course of your first week, if you're lucky. That's because when you were dreaming up all the things that you want to do, you never took into consideration all the other much more important and time-sensitive things that you'll need to deal with as soon as you return back to the community. I've certainly been there and know from my own first day out experience that as much as I assumed that it would be the best day of my life, walking out of prison was anything but. Instead of feeling happy, excited, and overjoyed to be out, I felt super-anxious, overwhelmed, and admittedly even a little scared because of how mentally unprepared I was to jump right back into the world after spending years incarcerated.

Most ex-offenders who don't have a pre-established support network for when they're released think that they're all on their own, and that feeling of having to face everything alone can easily drive them to want to give up before they've even started and go back to what they know and are comfortable with – committing crimes and making money illegally. But you need to know that's not the case at all. Even without the support of family and friends, you won't have to go through your re-entry alone. Even though you may feel alone, frustrated, overwhelmed and angry throughout much of your re-entry, always remember that you never have to feel like you're doing it all by yourself. There is a whole network of help available to you once you are back on the streets if you want it. That being said, some may choose not to want help; and if that works for you, cool, but just remember that the only reason that you would be alone is if you choose to be alone.

"IF YOU WANT TO GO FAST, GO ALONE. IF YOU WANT TO GO FAR, GO TOGETHER."

Today, more than ever, there's so many different resources available to assist ex-offenders in their re-entry. Experienced in working with ex-offenders and other disadvantaged groups, these individuals and programs have lots of street smarts that can be of great benefit to you in finding a job and dealing with all of your other important re-entry challenges. One of the best examples of this is your Parole Officer (PO). Because of my own experience, I have found that your PO is an essential key to your re-entry success and really the only way possible for you to be successful on parole. Believe it or not, your PO will be one of the most influential players in your own re-entry game plan.

You have to put the effort into creating a good relationship with them, and it will take time. But once you earn their trust and show them that you are really serious about going down the right path and becoming successful, your PO can guide you in just about every aspect of what you will need to succeed.

There are so many government agencies, non-profit organizations, and faith-based groups that provide ex-offenders with all types of assistance, from housing, health care, and substance abuse counseling, to job training and employment. If you're reading this while you're still incarcerated, use this book and others like it in the law library, along with talking with your prison counselor, social worker, family and friends, to help you look up the various community organizations and programs so you can prepare yourself now for when you're released so that once you get out, you can literally hit the ground running.

CHAPTER 5

5. RE-ENTRY RESOURCE DIRECTORY

COMMUNITY BASED PROGRAMS AND SERVICES

Not all communities are alike when it comes to assisting ex-offenders. Some are well organized to assist ex-offenders, while others are not as focused on re-entry issues, or they just throw ex-offenders into already existing services designed to assist disadvantaged groups but not specifically ex-offenders. Ex-offenders living in Philadelphia, Chicago (Safer Foundation), New York City (Center for Employment Opportunities), and Baltimore (Mayor's Office of Employment Development), for example, can benefit greatly from local efforts to provide employment programs and services for ex-offenders.

Some of the programs, such as the Safer Foundation in Chicago, actually start in jail and state prisons and involve both pre and post-release services. Other communities have employment placement and training programs, such as One-Stop Career Centers, non-profit organizations such as Goodwill Industries, which increasingly serve ex-offenders along with other hard-to-employ individuals, including welfare recipients, recovering addicts, and people with disabilities. Many of these programs offer housing, health care, job training, transportation, and child-care services to individuals as well as financial incentives, such as bonding and tax credits, to employers who hire hard-to-employ individuals.

This section is designed to help you to both understand and navigate all of the many programs and services designed for ex-offenders both available locally in your community, city, and across the country. If you relocate to Chicago or New York City, you'll find programs and services that deal with the immediate and long-term needs of ex-offenders: financial assistance, housing, short-term jobs, training, job placement, and job retention. Other communities such as Baltimore and Philadelphia may have a loose coalition of government agencies, non-profit organizations, programs, and churches focused on ex-offender re-entry and employability issues.

In many other smaller communities, however, you may be on your own; these are the toughest communities for ex-offenders who need a support system beyond just family and friends to help them with their re-entry needs and challenges. But even the smallest, most rural, right-wing extremist anti-felon communities still offer some type of assistance for ex-offenders if you know where to look for them. That's exactly what this part is all about, to become aware of alternative programs and services available in your community and the ones in close-by surrounding areas such as One-Stop Career Centers, non-profit organizations, and churches that assist disadvantaged groups, specifically ex-offenders.

In the end, with close to 700,000 ex-offenders re-entering communities across the country each year, all communities deal with their share of ex-offenders, some more than others, and have organizations and programs set up to assist them. So let's focus on getting some new street smarts by helping you identify services, where to go, and who to contact for re-entry assistance.

STATE BY STATE DIRECTORY

ALABAMA

The Lovelady Center
7916 2nd Avenue South
Birmingham, AL 35206
(Phone) 205-833-7410
A very powerful organization for women who are released from prison. Lovelady is a very reputable center that provides support and help for ex-offenders.

Renascence
215 Clayton Street
Montgomery, AL 36104
(Phone) 334-832-1402
Very nice "halfway house" that provides an excellent re-entry program for ex-offenders.

ALASKA

Alaska Native Justice Center
3600 San Jeronimo Drive
Anchorage, AK 99508
(Phone) 907-793-3550
Adult re-entry services for ex-offenders

Partners for Progress
419 Barrow Street
Anchorage, AK 99501
(Phone) 907-258-1192
They provide comprehensive re-entry support including employment services, transitional housing assistance, counseling and mentoring.

ARIZONA

Pueblo Community Services
4501 E. 5th Street
Tucson, AZ
(Phone) 520-546-0122
Welcomes men, women, and families re-entering the community from incarceration, military services, hospitalization treatment – people with a strong desire to change the course of their lives. This is a wonderful organization for ex-offenders.

CASS
230 S. 12th Avenue
Phoenix, AZ   85007
(Phone) 602-256-6945, x1100
Emergency shelter and job placement

ARKANSAS

Arkansas Community Center
Two Union National Plaza
105 W. Capitol Avenue
Little Rock, AR 72201
Offers a wide variety of help and programs for those re-entering society.

Our House
P. O. Box 34155
Little Rock, AR 72203
(Phone) 501-374-7383
Three housing programs that are designed to encourage sustainability. All residents must be willing and able to find and maintain a full-time job.

CALIFORNIA

A Brighter Day
264 S. La Cienega Blvd., Ste. 151
Beverly Hills, CA 90211
Free housing, new start program.

Clean 360

4107 Broadway
Oakland, CA 94611
(Phone) 510-451-0570
Help with employment and employment skills.

COLORADO

Colorado Gives

Community First Foundation
5855 Wadsworth Bypass, Unit A
Avada, CO 80003
Re-entry help and anti-recidivism programs.

FOCUS RE-ENTRY

4705 Baseline Road
Boulder, CO 80303
Mentoring program whose mission is to reduce recidivism and enhance community safety.

CONNECTICUT

EMERGE Connecticut

830 Grand Avenue
New Haven, CT 06511
(Phone) 203-562-0171
Transitional Workforce Development Program with the goal of providing recently released ex-offenders in the New Haven area with the opportunity to end the pattern of recidivism.

Family Re-Entry

75 Washington Avenue
Bridgeport, CT 06604
(Phone) 203-576-6924
Appears to be one of the best re-entry organizations in Connecticut.

DELAWARE

VOA: Delaware Valley
531 Market Street
Camden, NJ 08102
(Phone) 856-854-4660
Volunteers of America Delaware Valley's Re-Entry Services Division has a proven record of commitment, experience, versatility, and competence in operating community re-integration programs.

FLORIDA

Project 180
P. O. Box 25684
Sarasota, FL 34277-2684
(Phone) 941-677-2281
Re-entry help and support

Re-Entry Alliance Pensacola, Inc.
2615 West DeSoto Street
Pensacola, FL 32505
Services provided for Re-Entry, includes basic needs.

GEORGIA

NewLife Second Chance Outreach
4519 Woodruff Road, Unit 4 #344
c/o The Mail Room
Columbus, GA 31904
Local jobs and job-related services such as training and development.

HAWAII

Hope Services Re-Entry Services
296 Kilauea Avenue
Hilo, HI 96720
(Phone) 808-935-3050
Helps ex-offenders and felons with housing, jobs, and job skills.

IDAHO

Wellbriety for Prisons
912 12th Avenue South, Ste. 204
Nampa, ID 83686
(Phone) 208-461-3764
Re-entry information

ILLINOIS

Safer Foundation
571 W. Jackson Boulevard
Chicago, IL 60661
Help with GED exams, housing, jobs, and career skills for ex-offenders.

INDIANA

Brothers Keeper
P.O. Box 6164
Evansville, IN 47719
Addressing the needs of men as they return from prison to society with job search/employment, self-help skills, counseling, transportation, and healthcare.

New Leaf
1010 S. Walnut Street
Bloomington, IN 47401
(Phone) 812-355-6842
Programs for people both during and after incarceration that will reduce recidivism and build their capabilities and life skills.

IOWA

Re-Entry Aftercare
Altoona, IA 50009
(Phone) 515-230-8815
Educational and career support

Hope Ministries – Door of Faith
6701 SW 9TH
Des Moines, IA 50315
(Phone) 515-974-0545
Recovery program called Journey of Hope.

KANSAS

Oxford House for Men
Brian Holms
1739 N. Harvard
Wichita, KS 67208
Great re-entry program with housing.

Oxford House for Women
Stephanie King
704 S. Barlow Street
Wichita, KS 67207

ENTUCKY

Kentucky Re-Entry
(Phone) 502-782-9547
Helping returning citizens and justice-involved individuals on their journey to re-entry.

Goodwill Industries of Kentucky
909 E. Broadway
Louisville, KY 40204
(Phone) 502-585-5221
A program to help individuals by providing classes and job leads while helping maintain motivation during job search.

LOUISIANA

Baton Rouge DRC
2751 Woodale Boulevard
Baton Rouge, LA 70805
(Phone) 225-218-4636
Dedicated re-entry facilities with full-service programs.

Re-Entry Solutions for Louisiana
1617 Branch Street, Ste. 500
Alexandria, VA 71301
(Phone) 318-443-0189
Employment and housing help.

MAINE

Restorative Justice
P. O. Box 141
Belfast, ME 04915
(Phone) 207-338-2742
This re-entry program offers a wide variety of services and help.

MASSACHUSETTS

Dismas House
P. O. Box 30125
Worcester, MA 01603
A supportive community that provides transitional housing and services to former prisoners.

MICHIGAN

Michigan Prisoner Re-Entry Program
1333 Brewery Park Boulevard, Ste. 300
Detroit, MI 48207
(Phone) 517-372-3653
Helping prisoners return to the community prepared for success.

Michigan Works
2500 Kerry Street, Ste. 210
Lansing, MI 48912
Associate established in 1987 to support Michigan's workforce development.

MINNESOTA

Freedom Works
3559 Penn Avenue N
Minneapolis, MN 55412
(Phone) 612-522-9007
A Christian community providing housing and a pathway to meaningful employment.

MISSISSIPPI

New Way Mississippi
916 Inge Street
Jackson, MS 39203
Transitional and permanent housing acquisition, ongoing recover support services, transitional employment, and economic development opportunities.

Crossroads Outreach Ministries
P.O. Box 3075
Ridgeland, MS 39158
(Phone) 601-855-2332
Re-entry program for women.

MISSOURI

Power House
263 W. Morgan
Marshall, MO 65340
(Phone) 660-886-8860
Providing housing, transportation, and substance abuse recovery for offenders being released from prison.

Start Here
P. O. Box 220721
St. Louise, MO 63122
(Phone) 314-726-2092
An overall resource directory for re-entry.

MONTANA

Great Falls Rescue Mission
408 2nd Avenue South
Great Falls, MT 59405
(Phone) 406-761-2853
Recovery programs, shelters for both men and women, meals. Medical help and more within a Christian environment.

NEBRAKSA

Released and Restored
P. O. Box 22962
Lincoln, NE 68542
(Phone) 402-806-0565
Provides inmates and ex-offenders in Nebraska with the tools and support systems needed for learning how to live moral, ethical, and legal lives in our communities.

Re-Entry Alliance of Nebraska
Website: http://re-entrynebraska.org
Helping men and women make successful transitions back into the community by providing job training, life skills, transitional living, clothing and more. Unfortunately, the only contact information is a contact form on their website.

NEVADA

Hope for Prisoners
3430 E. Flamingo Road, Ste. 350
Las Vegas, NV 89121
(Phone) 702-586-1371
Helping men, women, and young adults re-enter society successfully.

Ridge House
900 West 1st Street, Ste. 200
Reno, NV 89503
(Phone) 775-322-8941
Counseling, job training, job placement, self-help support groups, mentoring services, and more.

NEW HAMPSHIRE

Alternative Solutions Associates, Inc.
(Phone) 413-626-7597
Email: kevin@alternativesolutionsassociates.com
Provides a range of services including re-entry program design, linkage to employment training and job development training and job development, casework and community linkage staff training, and more.

NEW JERSEY

NJ Re-Entry Corporation
398 Martin Luther King, Jr., Drive
Jersey City, NJ 07305
(Phone) 551-222-4323
Re-entry information for people living in or around Newark, NJ

Re-Entry Coalition of NJ
986 Broad Street
Trenton, NJ 08611
(Phone) 609-706-2684
An organization committed to offender rehabilitation.

NEW MEXICO

A Peaceful Habitation
P.O. Box 53516
Albuquerque, NM 87153
(Phone) 505-440-5937
A Christian ministry that provides transitional housing, support. and services to women re-integrating into society.

NEW YORK

Rising Hope, Inc.
P. O. Box 906
Croton Falls, NY 10519
(Phone) 914-276-7848
Rising Hope, Inc., provides one year of college-level courses to people incarcerated in New York State prisons.

Second Chance Re-Entry

244 5th Avenue, 2nd Floor
New York, NY 10001
(Phone) 212-726-2637
Our mission is to advocate for humane treatment and care to the proportionate segment of our society disabled and disenfranchised.

NORTH CAROLINA

CSI Resource Center Without Walls

P. O. Box 61114
Raleigh, NC 27661
(Phone) 919-715-0111, Ext. 239
Work with men and women in prison, former prisoners, people in transition and their families by providing small group trainings and individual mentoring in general life skills, leadership, entrepreneurship, financial literacy, and areas related to transforming back into family and community life.

Going Home Initiative

Department of Corrections-Research & Planning
2020 Yonkers Rd., 4221 MSC
Raleigh, NC 27699
(Phone) 919-716-3089
Creating a systemic pre-release, community transition and re-entry infrastructure. Creating the seamless system is a theme of the Going Home Initiative.

NORTH DAKOTA

Bismarck Transition Center

2001 Lee Avenue
Bismarck, ND 58504
(Phone) 701-222-3440, Ext. 101
A comprehensive community-based correctional program designed to help eligible, non-violent offenders transition back into the community. Provides essentials such as employment and housing once they are released into society.

Northlands Rescue Mission
420 Division Avenue
Grand Forks, ND 58201
(Phone) 701-772-6600
A place of rescue, relief, and restoration for all – no matter their needs or challenges

OHIO

Ohio Ex-Offender Re-Entry Coalition
OH Department of Rehabilitation and Correction-Court and Community
770 W. Broad Street
Columbus, OH 43222
(Phone) 614-752-0627
To ensure successful offender re-entry, reduce recidivism, and enhance public safety.

New Home Islamic Re-Entry Society
2302 Putnam Avenue
Toledo, OH 43620
(Phone) 419-283-2290
Providing a faith-based home for men who are homeless and/or who have recently been released from prison.

OKLAHOMA

The Oklahoma Partnership for Successful Re-Entry
P. O. Box 60433
Oklahoma City, OK 73146
(Phone) 405-615-6648
A statewide coalition of organizations working in the field of re-entry which is helping ex-felons reintegrate into society, especially after prison, but also including those re-entering from jail, probation, or moving here from out of state.

Turning Point
Community Action Agency of Oklahoma City
319 SW 25th Street
Oklahoma City, OK 73109
(Phone) 405-232-0199
Job readiness, resume preparation, interview preparedness, clothing and transportation allowance.

OREGON

Better People
4310 NE Martin Luther King, Jr., Blvd.
Portland, OR 97211
(Phone) 503-281-2663
An established employment and counseling program solely dedicated to helping individuals who have legal histories find, keep, and excel in well-paying jobs with fair, decent employers.

ROAR
(Re-Entry Organizations and Resources) Alliance
Mercy Corps Northwest
Skidmore Fountain Building, 43 SW Naito Pkwy.
Portland, OR 97204
(Phone) 503-896-5073
A collaboration of over 40 non-profit, faith-based and government agencies working to promote successful re-entry from incarceration to the community.

PENNSYLVANIA

Safe Haven Re-Entry Coalition (SHaRP)
P.O. Box 3477
Philadelphia, PA 19122
(Phone) 215-763-3079
A faith-based ministry committed to reaching out and empowering incarcerated men, women, and their family members through re-entry and life action skills to help reduce the recidivism pattern.

Stephen's Place, Inc
729 Ridge Street
Bethlehem, PA 18015
(Phone) 610-861-7677
Halfway House for non-violent adult males with a history of substance abuse who are coming out of prison and need a safe environment where they can reintegrate into society.

SOUTH CAROLINA

New Life Deliverance Worship Center Prison Ministry
361 Whitney Road
Spartanburg, SC 29303
(Phone) 864-285-1745
Helps men and women getting out of prison with clothing, food, job referrals, and transitional housing.

South Carolina STRONG
2510 N. Hobson Avenue
North Charleston, SC 29405
(Phone) 843-554-5179
To rehabilitate criminals and substance abusers and move people into economic self-sufficiency.

SOUTH DAKOTA

Center of Hope
225 E. 11th Street, Ste. 101
Sioux Falls, SD 57104
(Phone) 6605-334-9789
Providing for those who struggle including family concerns, relationship strains, addictions, financial concerns, joblessness, incarceration, hospitalization, spirituality questions, or feelings of helplessness.

TENNESSEE

Dismas House – Nashville
1513 16th Avenue South
Nashville, TN 37212
(Phone) 615-297-4511
A housing and intensive case management program that serves men who have recently been released.

Men-of-Valor Aftercare & Re-Entry
1410 Donelson Pike, Ste. B-1
Nashville, TN 37217
(Phone) 615-399-9111
Prisoners participating in Man of Valor are released into a year-long Aftercare/Re-Entry program aimed at giving them the support, skills, and accountability they need to succeed in the community.

TEXAS

Texas Offenders Re-Entry Initiative

P. O. Box 4386
Dallas, TX 75208
(Phone) 214-941-1325, Ext. 300
Committed to helping and improving the lives of people who have made mistakes in their past which makes their acceptance back into society a very difficult task. With TORI, you will find people who are ready to assist ex-offenders in making better decisions in order to avoid repeating an often dangerous and destructive life cycle.

SEARCH Homeless Services

2505 Fanin Street
Houston, TX 77002
(Phone) 713-739-7752
To engage, stabilize, educate, employ, and house individuals and families who are homeless.

UTAH

MentorWorks

Foundation for Family Life
1733 W. 12600 Street South, Ste. 230
Riverton, UT 84065
(Phone) 801-679-3921
This MentorWorks program has been developed to serve the needs of men and women as they are released from county or state correctional facilities and are now transitioning back into society.

VERMONT

Dismas of House Vermont

103 E. Allen Street
Winooski, VT 05404
(Phone) 603-795-2770
A supportive community for former prisoners transitioning from incarceration and university/college students who are also in transition with their lives. Living in a community accomplishes the Dismas mission of reconciliation. Community is fundamentally about relationships, and it is precisely the relationship between the offender and their community that is broken, first by the crime committed and subsequently by the resulting incarceration. In reconciliation, wholeness is restored to the former prisoner and to society.

Lamoille Restorative Center

P. O. Box 148
Hyde Park, VT 05655
(Phone) 802-888-0657
Males and females returning to the community from incarceration receive support services from a program coordinator and a team of volunteers. Offenders work with coordinators to develop a plan to re-integrate back into their community successfully.

VIRGINIA

Step Up, Inc.

5900 East Virginia Beach Boulevard, Ste. 102
Norfolk, VA 23502
(Phone) 757-588-3151
The purpose of STEP UP, Inc., is to help re-integrate offenders into society by providing them the knowledge, skills, and training they will need in order to make a successful transition from a correctional facility to the rest of their lives.

Total Action for Progress (TAP)

302 2nd Street SW
Roanoke, VA 24011
(Phone) 540-283-4903
Helps individuals and families achieve economic and personal independence through education, employment, affordable housing, and safe and healthy environments.

WASHINGTON

Conviction Careers

P. O. Box 432
Lynwood, WA 98046
(Phone) 866-436-1960
To fill a gap between employers and job seekers with criminal backgrounds. We know from Department of Corrections' studies that our program cuts the recidivism rate by 50%.

The STAR Project

321 Wellington Avenue
Walla Walla, WA 99362
(Phone) 509-525-3612
STAR's mission is to provide persons being released from incarceration with the essential tools to successfully re-integrate into the community as productive, contributing members of society.

WEST VIRGINIA

Covenant House
600 Shrewbury Street
Charleston, WV 25301
(Phone) 304-344-8053
To help people with the fewest resources meet their basic needs: food, clothing, and shelter. After 30 years, our core mission remains the same.

WISCONSIN

Fair Shake
P. O. Box 63
Westby, WI 54667
(Phone) 608-634-6363
Dedicated to reducing the recidivism rate through personal and community-focused ownership and engagement opportunities for inmates and former felons in connection with families, employers, property managers, corrections, and communities.

Project 180
728 N. James Lovell Street
Milwaukee, WI 53233
(Phone) 414-270-2957
A center for Self-Sufficiency (CFSS) program designed to improve employment outcomes for those who have been incarcerated and to lower their likelihood of re-incarceration. Project 180 participants are offered individualized services to help t5hem in a successful return home to Milwaukee.

WYOMING

Second Chance Ministries
201 W. Lakeway Road
Gillette, WY 82718
(Phone) 307-682-3148
To help men and women released from incarceration into Campbell County by providing re-entry assistance during the first four months after release to our clients and help rebuilding their lives through transformation of hearts and minds through Jesus Christ as demonstrated by our actions and kindness.

Transitional Housing & Self-Sufficiency Program CALC

211 W. 19th Street
Cheyenne, WY 82001
(Phone) 307-635-9291
Offers a variety of tools to help families and individuals recover from economic, medical, and other setbacks. Provides transitional housing to homeless individuals and families, as well as affordable housing to low-to-moderate income families.

HUD'S LOCAL OFFICE DIRECTORY

AK   HUD Anchorage Field Office
3000 C Street
Suite 401
Anchorage, AK 99503

AL   HUD Birmingham Field Office
417 20th Street North
Suite 700
Birmingham, AL 35203

AR   HUD Little Rock Field Office
425 West Capitol Avenue
Suite 1000
Little Rock, AR 72201-3488

AZ   HUD Phoenix Field Office
One North Central Avenue
Suite 600
Phoenix, AZ 85004

CA   HUD San Francisco Regional Office
One Sansome Street, Ste. 1200
San Francisco, CA 94104

CA   HUD Los Angeles Field Office
300 North Los Angeles Street, Ste. 4054
Los Angeles, CA 90012

CA   HUD Santa Ana Field Office
Santa Ana Federal Building
34 Civic Center Plaza, Room 7015
Santa Ana, CA 92701-4003

CO   HUD Denver Regional Office
1670 Broadway, 25th Floor
Denver, CO 80202-4801

CT   HUD Hartford Field Office
One Corporate Center
20 Church Street, 10th Floor
Hartford, CT 06103-3220

DC   HUD Washington, DC Field Office
820 First Street NE, Ste. 300
Washington, DC 20002-4205

DE   HUD Wilmington Field Office
800 North King Street, Ste. 307
Wilmington, DE 19801

FL   HUD Miami Field Office
Brickell Plaza Federal Building
909 SE First Avenue, Room 500
Miami, FL 33131-3028

FL   HUD Jacksonville Field Office
Charles East Bennett Federal Building
400 West Bay Street, Ste. 1015
Jacksonville, FL 32202

GA   HUD Atlanta Regional Office
Five Points Plaza Building
40 Marietta Street
Atlanta, GA 30303-2806

HI   HUD Honolulu Field Office
1003 Bishop Street, Ste. 2100
Honolulu, HI 96813-6463

IA   HUD Des Moines Field Office
210 Walnut Street, Room 937
Des Moines, IA 50309-2155

ID   HUD Boise Field Office
1249 S. Vinnell Way, Suite 108
Boise, ID 83709

IL   HUD Chicago Regional Office
Ralph Metcalfe Federal Building
77 West Jackson Boulevard
Chicago, IL 60604-3507

IN   HUD Indianapolis Field Office
Minton Capehart Federal Building
575 North Pennsylvania Street, Ste. 655
Indianapolis, IN 46204

KS   HUD Kansas City Regional Office
400 State Avenue, Room 200
Kansas City, KS 66101-2406
(Office also covers western portion of MO; for eastern portion of MO, see St. Louis, MO)

KY   HUD Louisville Field Office
Gene Snyder Courthouse
601 West Broadway, Room 110
Louisville, KY 40202

LA   HUD New Orleans Field Office
Hale Boggs Federal Building
500 Poydras Street, 9th Floor
New Orleans, LA 70130

MA   HUD Boston Regional Office
Thomas P. O'Neill, Jr., Federal Building
10 Causeway Street, 3rd Floor
Boston, MA 02222-1092

MD   HUD Baltimore Field Office
Bank of America Building, Tower II
100 South Charles Street, 5th Floor
Baltimore, MD 21201

ME   HUD Bangor Field Office
202 Harlow Street
Suite D2000
Bangor, ME 04401-4901

MI   HUD Detroit Field Office
McNamara Federal Building
477 Michigan Avenue
Detroit, MI 48226-2592

MN   HUD Minneapolis Field Office
212 Third Avenue South, Ste. 150
Minneapolis, MN 55401

MO   HUD St. Louis Field Office
1222 Spruce Street, Ste. 3.203
St. Louis, MO 63103-2836
(Office covers eastern portion of MO; for western portion of MO, see Kansas City, KS)

MS   HUD Jackson Field Office
Dr. A.H. McCoy Federal Building
100 West Capitol Street, Rom 910
Jackson, MS 39269-1096

MT   HUD Helena Field Office
Paul G. Hatfield US Courthouse
901 Front Street, Ste. 1300
Helena, MT 59626

ND   HUD Greensboro Field Office Asheville Building
1500 Pinecroft Road, Ste. 401
Greensboro, NC 27407-3838

ND   HUD Fargo Field Office
657 Second Avenue North, Room 366
Fargo, ND 58108-2483

NE   HUD Omaha Field Office
Edward Zorinsky Federal Building
1616 Capitol Avenue, Ste. 329
Omaha, NE 68102-4908

NH   HUD Manchester Field Office
Norris Cotton Federal Building
275 Chestnut Street, 4th Floor
Manchester, NH 03101-2487

NJ   HUD Newark Field Office
One Newark Center
1085 Raymond Boulevard, 13th Floor
Newark, NJ 07102-5260

NM   HUD Albuquerque Field Office
500 Gold Avenue SW, 7th Floor, Ste. 7301
Mailing Address: P.O. Box 906
Albuquerque, NM 87103-0906

NV   HUD Las Vegas Field Office
302 East Carson Street, 4th Floor
Las Vegas, NV 89101-5911

NY   HUD New York Regional Office
Jacob K. Javits Federal Building
26 Federal Plaza, Ste. 3541
New York, NY 10278-0068

NY   HUD Albany Field Office
52 Corporate Circle
Albany, NY 12203-5121

NY   HUD Buffalo Field Officer
300 Pearl Street, Ste. 301
Buffalo, NY 14202

OH   HUD Cleveland Field Office, North Point Tower
1001 Lakeside Avenue, Ste. 350
Cleveland, OH 44114

OH   HUD Columbus Field Office Bricker Federal Building
200 North High Street, 7th Floor
Columbus, OH 43215-2463

OK   HUD Oklahoma City Field Office
301 NW 6th Street, Ste. 200
Oklahoma City, OK 73102

OK   HUD Tulsa Field Office
110 West 7th Street, Ste. 1110
Tulsa, OK 74119

OR   HUD Portland Field Office
Edith Green-Wendell Wyatt Federal Office Building
1220 SW Third Avenue, Ste. 400
Portland, OR 97204-2825

PA   HUD Philadelphia Regional Office
The Strawbridge Building
801 Market Street, 12th Floor
Philadelphia, PA 19107

PA   HUD Pittsburgh Field Office
William Moorhead Federal Building
1000 Liberty Avenue, Ste. 1000
Pittsburgh, PA 15222-4004

RI   HUD Providence Field Office
380 Westminster Street, Ste. 547
Providence, RI 02903

SC   HUD Columbia Field Office
Strom Thurmond Federal Building
1835 Assembly Street, 13th Floor
Columbia, SC 29201-2480

SD   HUD Sioux Falls Field Office
4301 West 57th Street, Ste. 101
Sioux Falls, SD 57108

TN   HUD Nashville Field Office
Historic U.S. Customs House
701 Broadway, Ste. 130
Nashville, TN 37203

TN   HUD Knoxville Field Office
John J. Duncan Federal Building
710 Locust Street SW, 3rd Floor
Knoxville, TN 37902-2526

TN   HUD Memphis Field Office
200 Jefferson Avenue, Ste. 825
Memphis, TN 38103-2389

TX   HUD Fort Worth Regional Office
307 W. 7th Street, Ste. 1000
Fort Worth, TX 76102

TX   HUD Fort Worth Field Office
307 W. 7th Street, Ste. 1600
Fort Worth, TX 76102

TX   HUD Houston Field Office
1331 Lamar Street, Ste. 550
Houston, TX 77010

TX   HUD San Antonio Field Office
Hipolito Garcia Federal Building
615 East Houston Street, Ste. 347
San Antonio, TX 78205-2001

UT   HUD Salt Lake City Field Office
125 South State Street, Ste. 3001
Salt Lake City, UT 84138

VA   HUD Richmond Field Office
600 East Broad Street, 3rd Floor
Richmond, VA 23219-4920

VT   HUD Burlington Field Office
95 St. Paul Street, Ste. 440
Burlington, VT 05401-4486

WA   HUD Seattle Regional Office
Seattle Federal Office Building
909 First Avenue, Ste. 200
Seattle, WA 98104-1000

WI   HUD Milwaukee Field Office
310 West Wisconsin Avenue, Ste. 950
Milwaukee, WI 53203-2289

WV   HUD Charleston Field Office
414 Summers Street, Ste. 110
Charleston, WV 25301

WY   HUD Casper Field Office
150 East B Street, Room 1010
Casper, WY 82601-7005

STATE RE-ENTRY LISTINGS

G.R.O.W.N.
8410 Bustleton Avenue, Ste. 2
Philadelphia, PA 19152
(Phone) 267-694-1003
Website: www.wearegrown.org

Pennsylvania Prison Society
245 N. Broad Street, Ste. 300
Philadelphia, PA 19107-1518
(Phone) 215-564-6005

PENNSYLVANIA OFFICES OF VOCATIONAL REHABILITATION
Website: www.dli.pa.gov.ovr
The Office of Vocational Rehabilitation (OVR) serves people who have disabilities that present a substantial impediment to employment. Services are provided to individuals, including those who are returning to society from prison, to prepare for, secure, retain, advance in or regain employment.

Harrisburg Office
Forum Place
655 Walnut Street, 8th Fl
Harrisburg, PA 17101
(Phone) 717-787-7634

Philadelphia Office
801 Market Street, Ste. 6043
Philadelphia, PA 19107
(Phone) 215-560-1900

Pittsburgh Office
531 Penn Avenue
Pittsburgh, PA 15222
(Phone) 392-4950

Reading Office
3602 Kutztown Road, Ste. 200
Reading, PA 19605
(Phone) 610-621-5800

Wilkes-Barre Office

8 West Market Street, Ste. 200
Wilkes-Barre. PA 18701
(Phone) 570-826-2011

NATIONAL RE-ENTRY DIRECTORY

Affordable Homes Program (AHP)

Center for Employment Opportunities (CEO)

Citizens United for Rehabilitation of Errants (CURE)

www.curenational.org
A prisoner advocacy group with chapters in all 50 states

Felony Record Hub

www.felonyrecordhub.com
Felony Record Hub is a national website that provides formerly incarcerated people
with a wide range of resources, such as employment, legal guidance, housing assistance, and more.

Friends Outside

www.Friendsoutsideinscc.org
Chapters nationwide offering services to currently and formerly incarcerated people.

Helpforfelons.org

Jobsforfelonshub.com

Homelessshelterdirectory.org

Transitionalhousing.org

Housingassistanceonline.com

HUD Rental Assistance/Housing Choice Voucher Program

Kintock Group, Inc., Employment Resource Center

Incarcerated Veterans Transition Program (IV-TP)

Low Income Housing – US

Rental Assistance

National H.I.R.E. Network

www.hirenetwork.org

A great resource to begin with on your journey of re-entering into the world. It doesn't get much better: their website and interactive map of helpful re-entry information and resources in your particular state. The H.I.R.E. Network stands for: National Helping Individuals with criminal records Re-Enter through Employment Network. This is one of the most comprehensive and important state-by-state clearinghouses for identifying state and local re-entry resources. Established in 2001 by a non-profit organization, the H.I.R.E. Network is a one-stop shop for locating some of the best re-entry resources in each state.

National Re-Entry Resource Center through the Council of State Government Justice Center

www.csgjusticecenter.org/nrrc

Phoenix House Foundation

www.phoenixhouse.org

Provides comprehensive rehabilitation services to men, women, and children in more than 100 local centers in 9 states. (CA, FL, TX, NY, MA. MN, RI, NH, VT) Services include transitional housing, vocational training, life skills development, drug and alcohol programs and groups.

PrisonFellowship.org

CatholicCharitiesUSA.org

Reentrycentral.org
www.Ex-offender re-entry.org

Striveinternational.org

Volunteers of America Correctional Re-Entry Services

The Clean Slate Clearinghouse

National Reentry Resource Center
c/o CSG Justice Center
22 Cortlandt St, 22nd Floor
New York, NY 10007

The Next Step

www.thenextstep99.com

Dedicated exclusively to providing quality job opportunities to ex-offenders. They work to help ex-offenders find jobs across the U.S.

Annie E. Casey Foundation

www.aecf.org

This foundation is very much focused on improving the lives of children, families, and communities across the United States. One of its important focuses is on reforming the juvenile justice system. It conducts studies and pilot projects aimed at developing effective models that can be replicated across the country. It's especially noted for its Juvenile Detention Alternative Initiatives (JDAI) reform model that has been implemented in more than 250 U. S. counties as well as several intensive projects to help states and localities analyze and reorient their juvenile justice policies away from incarceration. Its groundbreaking study, ***No Place for Kids: The Case for Reducing Reliance on Juvenile Incarceration*** has proven that the current system of youth incarceration is dangerous, ineffective, obsolete, wasteful, and unnecessary, with no net benefit to public safety.

Catholic Charities

www.catholiccharitiesusa.org

Catholic Charities is all about caring for society's most vulnerable populations and communities. It's one of the nation's largest social service networks and outreach programs, the domestic missionary arm of the U.S. Catholic Church. Emphasizing safety, security, social justice, and caring for those in need, Catholic Charities consists of 164 member agencies serving 2,631 locations in the United States. It's devoted to helping individuals, families, and communities, from providing disaster relief, to promoting poverty reduction through research and legislative reform. Emphasizing the importance of marriage and families, its mission is to help those in need – poor, homeless, disabled, distressed, children, teens, single mothers, ex-offenders, immigrants, seniors – with food, shelter, education, training, financial security, healthy lifestyles, counseling, and adoptions.   In many communities, Catholic Charities is very much involved in operating ex-offender programs as well as substance abuse, mental health, transitional housing, and restorative justice programs. They are involved with prison ministries, support chaplains, and are advocates for juvenile justice, prison reform, and abolishing capital punishment.   Often working on the margins of society, these agencies operate child development centers, food pantries, refugee resettlement programs, housing projects, and senior centers.

Ex-Offender Re-Entry

www.exoffenderreentry.com

This is my gateway website to hundreds of ex-offender re-entry and related resources that we both publish and distribute. It's literally a one-stop shop for prison survival and ex-offender re-entry materials, with an emphasis on finding employment. The site pulls together the largest collection of books, pocket guides, DVDs, curriculum programs, assessment instruments, games, pamphlets, and workbooks relevant to ex-offenders and correctional administrators which are available through Impact Publications – www.impactpublications.com. If you're looking for specific resources and we don't have them, give us a call, and we'll most likely be able to locate what you need or at least advise you where to go. 1-800-361-1055. This site also includes links to other re-entry-related resources.

Food Pantries

www.foodpantries.org

This site includes a database of nearly 9,500 food pantries throughout the United States using an interactive U.S. map and state listings. New York State, for example, alone has 1,205 food pantries listed. The entries include descriptions and hours (usually limited) for food pantries. Some of the large food pantries, such as SERVE in Virginia, are also multifaceted public assistance groups that also provide emergency shelter for families and individuals, emergency assistance for utility, rent, water, and gas payments; access to free and reduced cost dental and specialty medical care; early Head Start programs; and job skills and life skills training and support.

Free Medical Clinics/Camps

www.FreeMedicalClinic.org or www.freemedicalcamps.com

This site includes links to hundreds of free temporary and permanent medical and dental clinics throughout the United States that cater to people without insurance or who lack independent financial means. It also includes clinics that may charge a small supportive fee or ask for a small donation. Some are only for low-income people, the homeless, or local community residents. Some specifically focus on HIV treatment and other specialized medical issues. In addition to the free clinic sources identified on this website, you're also advised to consider contacting your local county health department, religious organizations, charities, and doctors' and nurses' organizations, and doing Internet searches.

Free Public Assistance

www.freepublicassistance.com

For this site, free public assistance comes in many different forms: food banks, food pantries, homeless shelters, transitional housing, clinics and low-cost affordable treatment, rental assistance, welfare offices, drug and alcohol treatment, job training, and vocational training. The site includes an interactive state map and state listings for identifying public assistance programs and services nearest you.

Free Treatment Centers
www.freerehabcenter.com

This site presents a directory of free, sliding-scale, discounted, low-cost and Medicaid-sponsored treatment centers for individuals with substance abuse and addiction issues, especially drugs and alcohol but also gambling and other addictions. While the emphasis is on locating free treatment centers, the site also includes affordable treatment centers by state or ZIP code. The site also advertises a toll-free telephone number for speaking with an alcohol or drug abuse counselor. 1-800-607-2263.

Goodwill Industries International, Inc.
www.goodwill.org

Goodwill Industries is the nation's largest nonprofit provider of job training services with a network of 164 independent, community-based Goodwill Organizations and dozens of corporate and nonprofit partners, such as AT&T, Bank of America, Caterpillar, Microsoft, Sprint, Walmart, Annie E. Casey Foundation, Lumina Foundation for Education, and the Ford Foundation. Financed through a combination of donations, retail sales, and contracts and grants, Goodwill works with thousands of ex-offenders each year through its Second Chance Program (*2nd Chance @ Work*). A leader in the successful reintegration of ex-offenders into mainstream society, Goodwill operates several programs designed to help ex-offenders find and keep jobs, acquire safe and stable housing, and deal with substance abuse and health (both physical and mental) issues. To find a Goodwill location near you, visit their website and enter your ZIP code in its location search box.

Homeless Shelter Directory

www.homelessshelterdirectory.org

Competing with employment needs, housing ranks either number one or number two as the most pressing need for newly released ex-offenders. For ex-offenders who are destitute and living outside a safety net of welcoming family and friends, finding transitional housing can be extremely difficult and stressful for daily living. Newly released sex offenders in particular face barriers to finding such housing because of special restrictions placed on them due to their criminal conviction.

The online Homeless Shelter Directory is one of the most useful gateway websites for locating homeless shelters throughout the United States. This is not a dedicated ex-offender re-entry website, because homeless shelters cater to a much larger population of individuals and families who find domestic violence (battered women and children), homeless veterans, evicted renters and homeowners, and other people living on the streets (poor, disabled, and mentally ill.)

One of the nice features of this website is the colorful interactive search map that enables users to locate homeless shelters and service organizations throughout all 50 states.

Once you click on a relevant state, you can search for homeless shelters by city by entering the city name in a search box. This site also addresses many of the larger service and transitional issues affecting the homeless and needy, such as food stamps, soup kitchens, monetary assistance, free clinics (medical and dental), outreach centers, relief organizations, and low-cost or free addiction and rehab treatment centers. Since many ex-offenders may find themselves in a homeless or transitional housing situation immediately upon release, which also multiplies into other difficult living issues, (food, health, addiction treatment), this is an excellent gateway website that can help many ostensibly forgotten and invisible people who fall through the many expensive cracks in the American economy. The website also is a great resource for individuals wishing to volunteer at most of these shelters.

The site's top homeless shelter searches are for these seven communities: Chicago, Michigan, California, Orlando, New York City, San Diego, and Los Angeles. Such searches may mirror the major centers for such transitional housing.

HUD Rental Assistance

https://www.hud.gov/topics/rental assistance

This is the federal government's (Department of Housing and Urban Development) official housing portal for finding subsidized housing, public housing, and using the Housing Choice Voucher Program (Section 8). It includes a HUD Resource Locator for contacting HUD offices and programs throughout the country, including rural areas. It also includes useful information on a variety of housing subjects such as rental help in your state, housing counseling (call 1-800-569-4287), your housing rights and responsibilities, and buying versus renting.

Lionheart Foundation

www.lionheart.org

The Lionheart Foundation provides social emotional learning (literary) programs and rehabilitative services for incarcerated adults, at-risk adolescents, and teen parents. Its director, Robin Casarjian, developed three widely-used books and training programs that have been used by hundreds of correctional institutions and schools nationwide: *Houses of Healing, Power Source,* and *Power Source Parenting.* Lionheart's newly-designed website includes information on these resources, including video clips, as well as a very useful state-by-state listing of re-entry programs for ex-offenders, a bookstore, and blog.

Low Income Housing

www.lowincomehousing.us

This nationwide search site enables users, including seniors (62+ years old) to find affordable rentals and housing options for low-income families and individuals. Various sections focus on Section 8 housing programs, income-based/tax credit housing, low-income rentals, housing authorities, subsidized housing, and HUD, low-income, and income-based affordable apartments. Users can search for such housing by entering their state and ZIP code. The site includes published rental rates as well as useful phone numbers for calling the housing sources directly. This site also has tips on how to play the low income housing game, such as getting on as many apartment waiting lists as possible since the wait time can be extraordinarily long (years!).

Phoenix House Foundation

www.phoenixhouse.org

Focusing on substance abuse and mental health issues affecting millions of Americans, including the majority of ex-offenders, Phoenix House offers a variety of outpatient and residential treatment options through its many assessment, counseling, and treatment centers around the country. With nearly 50 years of experience, it currently operates 130+ programs in 13 states: California, Connecticut, Florida, Maine, Maryland, Massachusetts, Metro DC, New Hampshire, New York, Rhode Island, Texas, Vermont, and Virginia. In addition to standard assessment and treatment services, Phoenix House also offers the following programs: medical and dental care; psychiatric assessment, treatment, monitoring, and referral; family services; high school education and GED prep, vocational assessment, referral, training, and job placement; housing services, recreation, fitness, meditation, and yoga; horticulture therapy; animal therapy; and performing and visual arts therapy.

Prison Fellowship

www.prisonfellowship.org

Representing the world's largest faith-based outreach program for prisoners, ex-prisoners, and their families, the evangelical Prison Fellowship has been in operation for nearly 40 years. Founded by Chuck Colson, who was famous for his religious transformation while service a seven-month prison sentence for obstruction of justice (he was President Nixon's "hatchet man") in the Watergate scandal of 1974, Prison Fellowship is a Bible-based program designed to change prisoners' mindsets, turn around their lives, strengthen their families, and save their souls. The focus of the program is on Bible study, prayer, church leadership training, and church-based preparation for re-entry (life skills training, marriage, and parenting classes, and other skills training.)

Prisoner Re-Entry Institute

John Jay College of Criminal Justice
524 West 59th Street. New York, NY 10019. Main 212.237.8000.
Undergraduate Admissions. admissions@jjay.cuny.edu.212-237-8869.

This university-based institute, which is a leader in educating criminal justice professionals, primarily focuses on conducting policy-relevant research focused on the criminal justice system and re-entry policies. Its defined mission relates to these types of projects and activities.

- Developing, Managing, and Evaluating Innovative Re-Entry Projects.
- Providing Practitioners and Policymakers with Cutting-Edge Tools and Expertise.
- Promoting Education Opportunities for Currently and Formerly Incarcerated Individuals as a Vehicle for Successful Re-Entry and Reintegration
- Identifying "Pulse Points" and Creating Synergy Across Fields and Disciplines.

The Institute also functions as an information source for many media outlets that cover criminal justice and re-entry issues in the United States. Its director, Ann Jacobs, is frequently quoted in the media as an expert on re-entry.

Re-Entry Central

www.reentrycentral.org

The gateway site is especially useful for re-entry professionals who want to keep up with the latest news and developments on re-entry and related criminal justice issues. Functioning as an information clearinghouse, it includes many informative articles on re-entry. It also includes a library of archived articles, re-entry facts, videos, grants, upcoming events, and links. Annual subscriptions cost $35 for individuals and $100 for organizations.

Rental Assistance

This site functions as an online directory to nearly 3,400 government, nonprofit, and charitable rent assistance programs throughout the United State relevant to single mothers, the elderly, and those considered to be low-income individuals and families with housing needs. You can locate such programs and services by using the site's interactive map of the U.S. as well as enter ZIP codes in its search box. Since each organization listed has its own eligibility rules and conditions, you'll need to complete their online registration forms or call them. Rental Assistance also tries to keep in touch with users through its Facebook page: www.facebook.com/Rent-Assistance274391785999/.

Salvation Army

www.salvationarmyusa.org/usn/prison-ministries

The Salvation Army is very active in working with prison, probation, and parole officials through its prison ministries programs. In some areas, prisoners are paroled to the direct custody of The Salvation Army. Re-entry-related services include Bible correspondence courses, pre-release job training programs, and employment opportunities. Most of The Salvation Army's efforts are handled through its Adult Rehabilitation Centers and Harbor Light Centers, which function as halfway houses for ex-offenders who participate in work release programs. The **Adult Rehabilitation Centers** (ARCs) provide spiritual, social, and emotional assistance to men and women who have difficulty coping with personal problems and providing for themselves. The Centers offer residential housing, work, and group and individual therapy to prepare them for re-entry into society and return to gainful employment.

STRIVE

www.striveinternational.org

Operating since 1984, this East Harlem-based employment and training program for poor people and disadvantaged groups now operates in 20 cities nationwide and in five cities overseas. It helps people with significant barriers to employment, including those with rap sheets, receive the necessary training and support they need to find jobs and achieve economic self-sufficiency. Look for their operations in Boston, New York City, Yonkers (NY), White Plains (NY), Mount Vernon (NY), Hartford (CT), Bridgeport (CT), Philadelphia, Atlanta, Baltimore, Washington, DC, Greenville (NC) New Orleans, Flint (MI), Chicago, and San Diego. They also operate in London and four locations in Israel (Jerusalem, Tel Aviv, Beer Sheva, and Haifa).

Temporary Cash Assistance for Needy Families
www.Tanf.us

Need cash to tide you over in a rough patch of your family's life? This government resource (Office of Family Assistance, U.S. Department of Health and Human Services), an informational website that is not an official government website, provides cash assistance for pregnant women and families with one or more dependent children who need help in paying for food, shelter, utilities, and expenses other than medical. As its name suggests, Temporary Cash Assistance for Needy Families, TANF, this is a temporary program. It helps families become self-sufficient, offers preventative measures for out-of-wedlock pregnancies, encourages two-parent families, dispenses food stamps (SNAP benefits), and assists with job preparation. Rather than use payday loan services, which can charge up to 600% annual interest, families that participate in the TANF program can avoid such debilitating financial obligations. The site includes a TANF program state map for finding the TANF program nearest to your location. Families can receive up to 60 months of TANF benefits over their lifetime. To be eligible for this program, you must be a U.S. citizen, have a Social Security number, and meet certain income requirements.

The Center for Employment Opportunities
www.ceoworks.org

Operating transitional jobs programs for more than 30 years, the Center for Employment Opportunities annually offers life skills education, transitional employment, job placement, and post-placement services to more than 3,000 ex-offenders (disproportionately black and Hispanic) returning to New York City as well as to others under community supervision. Its model work experience program – the Neighborhood Work Project (NWP) provides participants with immediate, paid, and short-term employment while they take part in a program to develop skills for rejoining the workforce and restarting their lives. Much of CEO's focus is on the most at-risk populations, especially young adults ages 18-25, who have limited work experience and face strong barriers to entering the workforce. The program provides an intensive four-day job readiness workshop that deals with resume writing, job search skills, interview preparation, dress, and discussing one's conviction and incarceration. It also assesses individual needs for support services such as housing, clothing, childcare, transportation, and documentation. Participants undergo vocational assessment (reading, math, job-related skills) develop an employment plan, regularly meet with a job coach, and receive paid transitional employment

The Fortune Society

http://fortunesociety.org

Operating since 1967, The Fortune Society primarily focuses on helping ex-offenders successfully re-enter society. Servicing approximately 4,500 men and women in three primary locations in New York City, it focuses on various re-entry services: housing, employment, education, family, mental health, substance abuse treatment, and health. Many of The Fortune Society's approaches to re-entry have become models for other programs nationwide. The Society produces several useful re-entry publications (*The Fortune News,* special reports, and toolkits) that can be downloaded from their website. A highly respected re-entry organization that also promotes criminal justice education and reform through a policy center dedicated to its founder, David Rothenberg Center for Public Policy (DRCPP) which focuses on changing counterproductive laws and policies that create barriers to successful community re-entry.

The Safer Foundation

www.saferfoundation.org

Safer Foundation is truly a hands-on re-entry organization that has helped thousands of ex-offenders reclaim their lives by helping them find and keep jobs (the key to re-entry success) and adjust to life in the outside world. Primarily focusing on employment and re-employment of ex-offenders in northern Illinois (primarily Chicago) and the Quad Cities region of Iowa, the Safer Foundation is one of America's largest not-for-profit providers of such services. Its evidence-based programs address barriers to employment and include pioneering programs designed for youth and adults with criminal records. It also offers intensive case management and prevention education as well as promotes supportive services and other ancillary services. Each year, it helps more than 4,000 ex-offenders find employment through its various programs. The Foundation's website includes useful re-entry and criminal justice resources, news, success stories, eligibility requirements, videos, and audiences.

The Urban Institute

www.urbaninstitute.org

Operating since 1968, The Urban Institute has been conducting policy research on America's criminal justice system for decades. Combining the rigor of academic research and analytical skills with the practical street-level operations of policymakers, community leaders, and practitioners, The Urban Institute serves as a research powerhouse focused on a variety of urban issues, including the criminal justice and re-entry systems. A leading policy development and think tank headquartered in Washington, D.C., conducts numerous studies relating to incarceration and re-entry, including program evaluations. It analyzes crime trends, evaluates prevention initiatives, examines emerging criminal justice technologies, and recommends solutions to criminal justice system issues facing neighborhoods, cities, states, and the federal government. The **Crime and Justice** section of the Institute's website includes information on its activities as well as a synopsis of its many relevant research reports. Among its 11 different policy centers, the Institute's **Justice Policy Center** focuses on developing strategies for combating crime and promoting public safety.

The Vera Institute of Justice

www.vera.org

This is one of America's most respected institutes for criminal justice reform. Operating for more than 50 Years, the Vera Institute of Justice has been an innovative non-partisan, nonprofit center focused on improving the criminal justice system through research, demonstration projects, and technical assistance. Headquartered in New York City, it has offices in Washington, D.C., New Orleans, and Los Angeles and operates throughout the United States and abroad. Its specialized centers and programs focus on the following: immigration and justice, sentencing and corrections, victimization and safety, youth justice, family justice, prosecution and racial justice, and substance use and mental health. It partners with foundations, government officials, and community organizations at the local, state, federal, and international levels to improve criminal justice and safety systems. Its numerous successful demonstration projects have been adopted by governments, with 17 being incorporated as independent nonprofit organizations. Its recent study of jail trends in the United States (trends.vera.org) has raised some troubling questions about the unexpected and largely unexplained growth of incarceration in rural areas.

Transitional Housing
www.transitionalhousing.org

This site represents the Web's largest directory to transitional housing with a database of nearly 5,500 shelters nationwide. Most transitional housing is designed for people in crisis, such as the working homeless and victims of domestic violence. Transitional housing is normally for a limited period, usually from two weeks to 24 months.

This database is easy to use. Just enter your desired ZIP code in the search box, and the site will generate a list of transitional housing contacts in your search area. From there, you can contact the provider for detailed information on availability, qualifications, etc.

The site also offers related supportive services for those who need to live more independently, such as sober, detox, and drug treatment and addiction rehabilitation services. It advertises a toll-free number (1-800-334-8893) that connects with an alcohol or drug abuse counselor.

Volunteers of America
Correctional Re-Entry Services
www.voa.org/correctional-re-entry-services

VOA has been a pioneer in offering re-entry services to ex-offenders ("the formerly incarcerated") for 119 years. Today, it remains a major player in the re-entry field. Indeed, it operates a variety of halfway houses, work-release programs, day reporting diversion and pre-trial services, residential treatment, family support, and dispute resolution and mediation services. Its website includes a useful search function for locating re-entry services across the country by entering ZIP codes.

FREE MONEY & POSSIBLE HELP UPON RELEASE

Benefits available to former inmates
(Including those in a halfway house)

Social Security Office
Welfare Department
State Rehabilitation Office

WHAT DO I DO? WHO DO I TALK TO? WHERE DO I GO?
Go immediately to the nearest Social Security Office and ask to speak to a counselor so that you can apply for Social Security Insurance Emergency Supplemental Benefits of $1,500.00. Explain that you are emotionally and mentally unprepared to hold a job. Show them your parole or mandatory release papers in order to prove that you are just out of prison.
Note: You should check within 72 hours.

While at the office, fill out the necessary forms for the $310.00 monthly disability benefit for every month you were incarcerated.
Now go to the nearest Welfare Department Office and apply for General Relief. Again, show them your paroled or mandatory release papers as proof that you are just out of prison.

Tell them you need Financial Assistance immediately. A check should be issued to you within two (2) hours. It should be for approximately $150.00. Do not forget to get your food stamps while you are there. You should receive about $110.000 worth. While you are there, be sure to obtain your Medical Card for Health Protection Benefits. Note: This card can be used at any doctor's or dentist's office.

DO THIS WITHIN THE NEXT TEN DAYS!!!!!
Go to the State Rehabilitation Center where you can apply for various Federally Funded Loans and Grants. If you want to start a small business, make a list of the approximate costs of all the equipment you will need (tools, work clothes, etc.) and estimate for about how much operating cash you will need to start up the business until it begins to make a living for you. They may loan up to $50,000.

If you need to be BONDED for employment by a private employer, you can obtain the bond from any U.S. District Court. Go to the Probation & Parole Department.

SUPPLEMEMTAL SOCIAL INCOME (S.S.I.) can best be described as a form of welfare that is paid through the SOCIAL SECURITY OFFICE. Unlike Social Security benefits, there is no need

to qualify as far as your past income is concerned. You AUTOMATICALLY QUALIFY for S.S.I. because you are unemployed and considered to be to be disabled. Be sure that you understand the situation concerning your disability.

Federal legislation, at this time, documents recognition that you are an ex-offender to the fact that you have an emotional problem. Basically, the government has declared that had you not had this emotional problem, you would have been able to conform to the rules of society, thus preventing your commission of a federal crime. Regardless of whether or not you feel or accept the fact that you as an ex-offender do in fact have this emotional problem, it is considered by both Federal and State Rehabilitation Commissions to be a disability. According to the current policies, mental and emotional problems constitute a 100% disability, and you will be considered to have this disability until you have become a "productive member" of society. The whole purpose of Supplemental Social Income (S.S.I.) is to help you as a recently released ex-felon by relieving part of the economic pressure you will be facing as you re-enter society and try to re-establish yourself as a productive member of your communities.

After you're released, you as a parolee or otherwise, will qualify for assistance of up to $310.00 per month. Although you do qualify, you will only be able to receive your S.S.I. benefits while you are still in prison waiting to be released. You, by law, have only 30 hours after you are released to reach the nearest Social Security Office and submit your application. It is necessary that you take the required steps before your release date and apply for these benefits, or you will lose the opportunity to take advantage of S.S.I., so 90 days prior to your release, send in your application to be processed. You should have a check waiting for you in the amount of $930.00. Supplemental Social Income is covered under United States Law 42 U.S.C., 1383 (c); 20 CFR 416.305.

1. Ninety (90) days before release, write a letter to the Social Security Office. They will send you a five (5) question application. Fill it out as accurately as possible, and then return it to the Social Security Office nearest you.
2. When your application is processed, you will get a check for three (3) months totaling $930.00 at $310.00 each.
3. You can also call the Food Stamp Office's Hot-Line and get $80.00 worth of food stamps when you go to the Department of Social Services. Also, you can apply for a full Food Stamp Grant. This will bring the total to $160.00
4. You are qualified because you are on the S.S.I. The Welfare Department will automatically send you $228 per month for financial assistance and utilities. S.S.I. is the same in each state.

(a) Go to the Department of Vocational Rehabilitation because you are on S.S.I.

(b) A convicted felon is a depressed minority. You also qualify for a certain benefit package. The amount of this benefit is $1,900 to be used for a down payment on a car. The car must be needed to go back and forth to work.

(c) Also, you received a $300 check for clothing for the job and another $400.00 check for street clothes, and finally, a $400 check for tools. These are GRANTS, NOT LOANS, so they do not have to be paid back.

(d) S.B.A. has programs for ex-felons. You are qualified to receive a Small Business Administration loan of up to $50,000.

CHAPTER 6

6. APPELLATE 225 CHECKLIST
Pre & Post Conviction Appeals

Failure to Investigate or Prepare

- In general
- Expert witnesses
- Prosecution witnesses
- Alibi witnesses
- Impartial witnesses
- Intoxicated witnesses
- Character witnesses
- Potentially corroborating witnesses
- Purported admission by someone else
- Defendant's background and/or priors
- Co-defendant's background
- Defendant's prior statements
- Co-defendants prior statements
- Defendant's sanity
- For sentencing
- Mitigating evidence
- Discovery materials
- Exculpatory evidence
- Information given the defendant by the prosecutor
- Defense to be presented
- Possible defenses
- The only conceivable defense
- Identification defenses
- By attorney's investigator
- Informant witnesses
- Entrapment witnesses
- Because the necessary testing was expensive
- Failure to investigate because defendant said not to
- Interstate agreement on detainers/speedy trial defense
- Police reports
- Voice exemplar

- Transcripts of previous testimony
- Search warrants
- Count to which plea is made
- Basic criminal procedure
- Recent developments in the law
- Cause and prejudice for failure to investigate the law may lie in the very novelty
- Scene of the crime
- Fingerprint evidence
- For penalty phase
- For penalty phase
- Disposition of earlier cases (charges, probation or parole)
- Insufficient time for retained counsel to prepare
- Non-strategic decision not to investigate
- Pre-trial claim of failure to investigate made by the defendant
- Last-minute appointment of counsel
- Failure to listen to the defendant's version of the case following improper procedures to secure the presence of a witness
- Counsel told the defendant that neither the defendant nor his lawyer was authorized to interview prosecution witnesses.

Failure to Interview

- Prospective defense witnesses
- Alibi witnesses
- Expert witnesses
- Expert witnesses on voluntary intoxication
- Expert witnesses on impotency
- Impartial witnesses
- Informant witnesses
- Prosecution witnesses
- Self-defense witnesses
- Entrapment witnesses
- The defendant

Plea Bargaining and Related Issues:

- Failure to communicate a plea offer
- Failure to give defendant a copy of the plea offer

- Extraordinary efforts by counsel at plea hearing to elicit an admission of guilty from his client
- Failure to communicate a counteroffer
- Failure to tell defendant of an offer of immunity

Erroneous Advice to Induce Acceptance of Plea Agreement

- Lying to the Defendant
- As to parole or probation
- As no sentence to be imposed
- Rushing into plea without investigation
- Plea not knowingly and intelligently made
- Improper pressure on defendant to plead guilty
- Despite a double jeopardy defense
- Plea urged by counsel biased against defendant
- Plea urged by counsel for the sake of a contingent plea agreement for a co-defendant
- Failure to fully explore plea possibilities
- Failure to advise defendant of the judge's change of mind
- Failure to advise of effect of plea on outstanding petition for habeas corpus
- Conflict of interest affecting plea negotiations
- As to ability to withdraw guilty plea afterward
- Misrepresentation of material facts
- Withholding material facts from defendant
- Failure to seek a plea agreement in Washington when efforts to deal with local U.S. Attorney fails.
- Because counsel is unprepared for trial
- Failure to explain the mens rea element of crime
- Erroneous advice to refuse plea agreement
- Failure to seek a plea bargain
- Failure to advise as to deportation consequences
- Failure to seek a judicial recommendation against deportation at sentencing
- Failure to research the law before plea
- Failure to realize the defendant was eligible for Young Adult Offender Treatment
- Inducement of guilty plea for the sake of counsel's relationship with the "federal people"
- Age and cultural differences between client and counsel
- Emotional involvement in the case as a reason for recommending against plea
- Pursuit of plea agreement as reason for lack of trial preparation
- Threat to pull bail as pressure on defendant to plead

- Attorney frustrated efforts to withdraw plea
- Failure to investigate defendant's competency before plea
- Delay by state in appointing counsel
- Failure to understand the consequences of withdrawing a plea
- Colorable claim of innocence required to vacate plea
- Judge in off-the-record plea discussions during trial
- Counsel's mistaken belief about the existence of a plea agreement with the prosecutor
- Failure to accurately calculate federal sentencing guidelines when advising defendant as to plea offer
- Attorney misinterpreted the indictment
- Failure to explain the risks and benefits of a plea offer

Pre-Trial Proceedings:

- Suppressing evidence
- Failure to explain the risks and benefits of a plea offer
- Failure to seek defendant's release on bail
- Failure to request time in which to review Jencks material
- Putting defendant on the stand at the detention hearing
- No counsel at preliminary hearing
- Failure to file a timely motion for substitution of counsel
- Failure to notify the court when differences arise between the defendant and counsel
- Failure to give notice of alibi defense
- Failure to secure expert testimony at government expense
- Counsel publicly chastised his client to the media
- Denial of a continuance as contributing to ineffectiveness of counsel
- Failure to advise co-counsel of the facts (which merited suppression of the confession)
- Improper waiver of the defendant's right to be present at a pre-trial deposition
- Failure to allege facts to establish standing at suppression hearing
- Erroneous legal advice resulting in loss of an absolute defense
- Failure to request a continuance
- Failure to challenge veracity of a search warrant application
- Failure to inform defendant that the judge knows of his criminal history before waiving the jury trial
- Failure to move for a severance of charges
- Improper procedures to secure a witness' presence
- Improper photo lineups

- Prejudicial publicity
- Competency hearings
- Standby counsel for a pro se defendant was ineffective
- Failure to cross-examine state's witnesses
- Failure to present rebuttal witnesses
- Defendant has a right to other counsel at a competency of counsel hearing
- Failure to attempt to enforce an agreement to admit polygraph results at trial
- Last minute substitution of appointed counsel

Motion Practice

- Failure to file motion for or to:
- Bail
- Dismiss
- Notice of alibi and disclosure of information
- Severance of defendants
- Suppression of evidence
- Continuance
- Mistrial
- Severance of charges
- Suppression of priors
- Suppression of confessions
- Suppression of witness identification
- Recess in which to review Jencks material
- Fundamental motions under local practice
- Failure to request rulings on pending motions
- Failure to move to suppress
- Inadequate motion for new trial

Jury Selection Proceedings

- Failure to challenge selection procedure
- In general
- For race and/or sex composition
- Failure to challenge jurors who are related to the prosecution team
- Failure to challenge jurors who are related to the victim
- Failure to move for exclusion of the jury pool during the presentation of irrelevant and prejudicial information
- "Perfunctory approach" to jury selection

- Failure to voir dire
- Failure to object to jurors who sat on an earlier jury in the same case

Conduct of the Trial

- Ambush by the government
- Failure to make an opening statement
- Failure to allow defendant to testify
- Failure to ask questions in proper form
- Failure to present defense chosen
- Failure to present defense promised in opening argument
- Failure to allow defendant to proceed pro se
- Failure to establish or maintain the requisite confidential relationship with client
- Failure to ask defendant critical questions on direct
- Failure to use impeachment evidence as directed by defendant
- Failure to raise collateral estoppel
- Failure to know the law
- Failure to exercise professional judgment on behalf of client
- Failure to notify the court when differences arise between defendant and counsel
- Failure to call witnesses
- In general
- Character, critical, or expert witnesses
- Failure to appreciate impact of prejudicial evidence
- Failure to interview prosecution witnesses so that they would be nervous during cross examination
- Failure to review Jencks material
- Failure to present medical testimony as to sanity
- Failure to impeach a witness
- Failure to request a mistrial
- Failure to obtain civilian clothing for the defendant
- Failure to request a continuance
- Failure to make an objection specifically requested by the defendant
- Failure to invoke the rule (excluding witnesses)
- Failure to correct prosecution's use of false statistics
- Failure to inquire into causal connection
- Failure to correct judge's response to jury query
- Failure to move for a severance
- Failure to subject prosecution's case to meaningful adversarial testing
- Failure to object based on currently evolving changes in the law

- Failure to move for mistrial when judge instructs as to parole consequences
- Failure to note, object to, or argue lack of corroborating evidence to an aggravating felony
- Calling a witness knowing he will invoke the 5th Amendment
- Counsel sleeping through the trial
- Counsel inattentive during trial
- Counsel intoxicated during trial
- Counsel removed himself in mid-case
- Counsel failing to participate in trial
- Counsel prevented from conferring with defendant
- Counsel lost important evidence
- Counsel did not understand only viable defense
- Counsel absent during deliberations and verdict
- Counsel concerned about his personal embarrassment
- Telling jury counsel is appointed
- Telling jury defendant is testifying against the advice of counsel
- General attitude of counsel
- Counsel misled defendant as to his intentions
- Counsel underpaid by the state
- Using bizarre, insane, or incredible defense
- Counsel deliberately made a sham and mockery of the trial
- Introduction of priors by defense counsel
- Opening the door for admission of defendant's confession
- Ignorance of the elements of the crime
- Eliciting needless but gruesome testimony
- Mere appearance of in-court effectiveness not enough
- Counsel ordered not to speak to client during recess
- Counsel ordered not to disclose identify of informant to defendant
- Counsel argued an inappropriate defense
- Cross-examination
- Denial of right
- Extensive cross is not automatically effective cross
- Failure to properly preserve error
- Failure to ask defendant where he was at time of crime when presenting an alibi defense
- Stipulating to non-existent priors
- Use of uncounseled priors as evidence
- Informing jury of sentence already imposed
- Failure to stipulate to a prior

- Lack of devotion to the interests of the accused
- Deliberate "screw up" in order to create error
- Putting defendant on the stand and having him admit to the elements of the offense
- Knowingly presenting false alibi witnesses
- Failure to attempt to enforce agreement to admit polygraph results at trial
- Agreeing to an instruction which advises the jury that the defendant was previously convicted of the same crime.
- Requesting an instruction which constructively amends indictment
- Government conduct affirmatively misled the defense
- Counsel provided the evidence necessary to fill in the gaps in the prosecution's case
- Failure to advise of consequences of testifying

Final Argument

- Incompetent summation
- Use of obscenities in final argument
- Counsel prevented from giving final argument
- Denial of the right to summarize
- Crucial misstatement of the evidence by defense counsel during final arguments
- Admission of guilt by counsel without defendant's consent
- Counsel admitted elements of the crime
- Telling the jury of the defendant's priors
- Allowing the prosecutor to describe the defendant's priors
- Telling jury the defendant is also accused of another crime
- Government "ambush" in final argument
- Failure to recognize the importance of the jury's questions
- Failure to object to prosecutorial illusions to defendant's failure to testify

Appeals

- Failure to give notice of appeal
- Failure to give notice of appeal on time
- Failure to advise defendant of the time limit for filing notice of appeal
- Consequences of filing an appeal past the deadline
- Failure to file a proper Anders brief
- Poorly written brief
- Refusal of counsel to file an appeal of Rule 11 FRCP grounds
- Briefing the case against client in Anders brief
- Failure to cooperate with replacement counsel

- Failure to advise defendant of rights concerning appeal
- Failure to advise defendant of right to appointed counsel on appeal
- Failure to file a timely brief because public defender is overworked
- Deceiving the defendant as to the existence of an appeal
- Refusal of trial counsel to turn over case files to post-conviction counsel
- Obligation of counsel to anticipate future developments in law
- Failure to appreciate risk of greater sentence if an appeal is filed
- Failure to advise the defendant of the risk inherent in the appeal
- Erroneous advice as to "risk" in appealing
- Failure to comply with state rules of procedure
- Failure to secure a complete transcript on appeal
- Failure of newly appointed counsel to contact defendant within time allowed to give notice of appeal
- Failure to advise defendant of a change in the law
- Failure to perfect appeal within a reasonable time
- A delayed appeal does not include the right to the benefit of superseded state law
- Dilatory prosecution of appeal can create a conflict of interest between defendant and counsel responsible for late appeal

Failure to Raise Issue on Appeal

- Ineffective trial counsel
- Because current state law is unfavorable
- Valid issues in general
- "A forgone ground upon which a new trial could have been obtained"
- Mental competency of defendant
- Prosecutorial vouching
- Prejudice is presumed from counsel's failure to file a non-frivolous appeal
- Under certain circumstances, counsel has a duty to discuss merits of appeal even though defendant has pled guilty
- Failure to ensure that defendant received appointed counsel on appeal
- Failure to advise defendant of right to appointed counsel on appeal
- Failure to raise a state law right on appeal in state courts

Failure to Offer Instructions

- Lesser included offense
- Accomplice
- Instructing the jury as to parole consequences

- Missing informal
- To disregard irrelevant prejudicial evidence overheard by the jury panel
- On trustworthiness of statements made by defendant
- On voluntary intoxication
- Self-defense
- No instructions at all
- Limiting instruction
- As to a mitigating circumstance
- Entrapment
- Offering an instruction which constructively amends the indictment

Sentencing

- Admission of aggravating factors by counsel without defendant's consent
- Admission of guilt by counsel without defendant's consent
- Failure to aid at sentencing
- Counsel acted as a mere spectator at sentencing
- Failure to pursue a judicial recommendation against deportation
- Failure to present mitigating evidence
- Failure to advise the court of its options under the Youth Court Act
- Failure to protect the defendant (by revealing his comments to the court)
- Failure to advise the jury that defendant had no prior criminal record
- Failure to advise the jury defendant's prior record was minor
- Failure to consult with defendant on Presentence Report
- Failure to object to the use of juvenile conviction, obtained without due process as prior
- Failure to object to an unconstitutional aggravating circumstance
- Failure to know the law with respect to sentencing
- Failure to present mitigating evidence because the defendant said not to
- Failure to attempt to humanize the defendant (in final argument at penalty phase)
- Dehumanizing the defendant (in final argument at penalty phase)
- Failure to object to ex-parte information provided to the court before sentencing
- Failure to obtain records of defendant's prior incarceration (to rebut prosecutor's argument in penalty phase)
- Failure to object to erroneous instructions at sentencing
- Failure to investigate or prepare for sentencing
- Unprofessional errors at sentencing
- Ineffective representation at sentencing
- Standby counsel does not qualify as assistance of counsel under the 6th Amendment

- Counsel asked the jury to spare defendant's life so that he could be used for medical experiments

Federal Sentencing Guidelines

- Failure to object to incorrect base offense level
- Failure to argue for a reduction in base offense level
- Failure to tell court of defendant's legitimate income
- Failure to consider prior convictions
- Priors may be challenged during sentencing proceedings

Post-Trial Proceedings

- Failure to help with a Rule 35 motion
- Anders requirements do not apply to state post-conviction proceedings
- Refusal of the court to appoint a psychiatrist to assist post-conviction counsel
- Failure to file brief in opposition to state's appeal of suppression order
- Defendant has a right to counsel during period after sentencing within which notice of appeal must be given
- Refusal of appointed counsel to advocate defendant's cause
- Failure to object to use of a non-qualifying prior conviction

Attorney's Personal Problems

- Death of counsel in mid-trial
- Disbarment
- Practicing law without a license
- Suspended from practice
- Fraudulent admission to bar
- Criminal exposure
- Counsel forced to give self-exculpatory testimony
- Grand jury subpoena of counsel
- Counsel being prosecuted in same court in another case
- Alzheimer's disease
- Mental instability
- Counsel mentally incapacitated and of unsound mind
- Attorney-client relationship no longer viable
- Lack of devotion to the interests of the accused
- Counsel racially prejudiced against the accused

- Drug usage
- Inattention
- Sleeping during trial
- Intoxication
- Counsel called as prosecution witness
- Fireworks between judge and counsel
- Acceptance of private payment by appointed counsel
- Concern about personal reputation or embarrassment
- Conflict of interest
- Attorney a doormat for the prosecutor's office
- Counsel unqualified to handle a criminal trial
- Lack of performance due to non-payment of fees
- Counsel claiming his own ineffectiveness
- Counsel had a "grandiose, perhaps even delusional" belief in her own abilities

Investigator Related Problems

- Counsel's obligation to independently verify investigator's conclusions
- Disclosure of confidential information by investigator to the prosecution
- Failure of investigator to proceed as directed
- Failure to send an investigator
- Counsel is required to do more than merely accept an investigator's statement that witnesses will not testify

Judge-Related Problems

- Counsel's obligation to independently verify investigator's conclusions
- Ordering counsel not to disclose identity of informant to his client
- Failure to seek disqualification of the judge
- Interference by judge with counsel's strategy
- Refusal to allow the defendant to proceed pro se
- Failure to inform defendant that the judge knows of his criminal history before waiving jury trial
- Failure to act when circumstances suggest an unseemly desire by the judge to rush resolution of the case
- Failure to prevent a conflict of interest
- Outrageous conduct by the judge
- Failure to correct judge's response to jury query

- Forcing defendant to proceed pro se or be bound by counsel's decision to testify in his own defense
- Judge participating in off-the-record plea discussions during trial
- "Sarcasm and pettiness" of the judge denied pro se defendant a fair trial

Defense Counsel's Conflict of Interest

- Previously prosecuted the defendant
- Previously represented the co-defendant
- Previously represented a key government witness
- Was influenced by co-defendant
- District court has wide discretion to refuse waivers from defendants
- Also represented victim in civil suit
- Was campaign manager for the prosecutor's election campaign
- Was executor of the murder victim's estate
- Was sexually involved with the defendant's fiancé
- Advised the defendant on how to avoid the money reporting laws in order to pay his fees
- Advised one client to act against the interests of another
- Failed to withdraw from representation of one of multiple defendants with conflicting interests
- Was also a target of prosecution
- Was preoccupied with preventing his own indictment in another case
- Had his own interest which conflicted with those of the defendant
- Showed partiality to one defendant over another
- Refused to let one co-defendant testify he had withdrawn from the conspiracy before others had completed it
- Worked against his client's interests
- Was paid by another target of the investigation who had conflicting interest
- Was an associate of counsel for a co-defendant with conflicting interests
- Was also counsel to the county where the defendant was being prosecuted
- Also represented defendant's employer
- Represented government witness in unrelated civil matter
- In his position as Justice of the Peace, issued the arrest warrant for the defendant
- Was told by judge at beginning of trial that he would be given a disciplinary hearing while jury deliberated
- Faced a conflict between surrendering more assets and getting a shorter term for defendant, or a longer term, thus preserving assets with which to pay his own fees
- Had the literary rights to client's life story

- Failed to fully explore plea negotiations due to conflict of interest
- Counsel claimed his own ineffectiveness
- Also represented co-defendants testifying against his client on trial
- Also represented co-defendants testifying against his client at sentencing
- Asked prosecutor to file increased charges against his client in order to motivate client to pay his fees
- Recruited client to sell drugs for him in exchange for legal fees
- Was target of undercover investigation in which government was using his client as informant
- Also represented the prosecutor in an unrelated civil matter
- Previously represented persons defendant is accusing of the crime
- Was partner in law firm defendant blamed for the offense
- Was placed in a conflict between his own personal interests and those of his clients by the actions of the judge
- Conflict of interest manifested at sentencing
- Was being sued by defendant
- Was waiting for employment by the prosecutor's office
- Was plea-bargaining for his own case at the same time was representing defendant on appeal
- Represented two or more co-defendants, one of whom as secretly a government informer
- Was alternate executor (to defendant) of deceased's estate
- Failed to request a continuance in order to cover up his own lack of pretrial preparation
- Perjured himself at evidentiary hearing
- Was facing disciplinary proceedings before the Bar
- Had financial interest in successful prosecution of his client
- Conspired with the government to cause client's arrest
- Judge should have prevented the conflict
- Defendant must be given opportunity to intelligently waive a conflict being urged by the government
- Pre-trial waiver of conflict was insufficient
- Pre-trial disqualification of defense counsel is not immediately appealable
- Appellate counsel sued by trial counsel for alleging ineffective assistance
- Dilatory prosecution of appeal caused actual conflict of interest between counsel and defendant
- Ineffective assistance at remand due to conflict of interest caused by suit against counsel
- Must actual prejudice be shown when an actual conflict exists?

- When defendants have timely objected to joint representation, they need not show an actual conflict of interest where the court failed to adequately inquire into the situation

Miscellaneous Listings

- Ineffective assistance in general
- ABA Code of Professional Responsibility, Canon 7
- Acceptance of private payment by appointed counsel
- Ambush by the government
- Bail
- Barring counsel from disclosing information to client
- Basing strategy on previously overturned law
- Claims of off-the-record promises must be resolved
- Collateral consequences justify relief
- Collateral estopped as a bar to use of evidence by prosecution
- Actual innocence: protections available in case of
- Colorable claim of innocence required to vacate plea
- Competency hearing
- Conflict of interest
- Consultation between defendant and counsel: denial of right to
- Counsel deploring crime and advocating maximum term at sentencing proceedings
- Counsel's testimony at the evidentiary hearing unworthy of belief
- Counsel's willingness to accept government's version of the facts of the case
- Cross-examination
- Collusion between counsel and prosecutor
- Cultural differences between attorney and client
- Cumulative effect of many errors: multiplicity of errors
- Defective prior felonies
- Delay by the state in appointing counsel
- Detention hearing
- Double jeopardy
- Erroneous information to induce a plea
- Erroneous stipulations
- Evidentiary hearings are required
- Expression of personal opinion of crime by defense counsel at the sentencing proceedings
- Facts are required to support an ineffective assistance claim
- Failure to advise client as to legal alternatives

- Failure to call witnesses because of weak prosecution case
- Failure to consult with the defendant
- Failure to do pre-trial discovery
- Failure to elicit crucial testimony from the defendant
- Failure to make informed evaluation of potentially viable defense
- Failure to prepare for trial
- Failure to research the law
- Failure to review prosecution's instructions
- Fingerprints
- Fundamental miscarriage of justice
- Gun powder residue
- I.A.D. (Interstate Agreement on Detainers)
- Improper argument
- Inattention of counsel
- Inexperience of counsel
- Inference of strategic reasons for trial counsel's failures, in the absence of on-the-record evidence to that effect, is improper
- It is an error to decide on basis of competing affidavits without a hearing
- Lack of diligence in seeking bail
- Lack of instructions as to separate counts
- Last minute appointment of counsel
- Legal standards to be applied in determining effectiveness of counsel
- Lesser included offenses
- Limited contact by counsel with defendant and his witnesses
- Literary rights
- Low payment as reason for lack of effort
- Maximum sentence recommended by defense counsel
- Mens rea (state of mind during offense)
- Mere appearance of in-court effectiveness
- Mishandling change of venue hearing
- Misleading the defendant on a matter central to defense strategy
- Multiple representation
- Multiplicity of errors
- Perfunctory representation
- Photo lineups
- Police statements cannot generally serve as an adequate substitute for a personal interview
- Pre-indictment right to counsel
- Prejudicial publicity

174

- Preliminary hearing
- Presumption of prejudice
- Private vs. appointed counsel, responsibilities of
- Probation revocation proceedings
- Procedural default
- Prosecutor later representing victim/plaintiff in civil suit
- Refusing to allow the defendant to testify
- Serious misunderstanding of the law
- Severance
- Sexual relations between counsel and defendant's fiancé
- Sham trial
- Shoe prints
- Single substantive error
- Speedy trial
- Speedy trial rights, insistence upon is not a waiver of effective counsel
- Standby counsel does not meet 6th Amendment standard for assistance of counsel
- Suit by defendant against counsel
- Suit by trial counsel against appellate counsel for alleging ineffective assistance of counsel
- Summation
- Supreme Court cases change the law of the case
- Trial in absence of the defendant
- Use of uncounseled prior felonies as proof of prior conspiracy
- Attorney-client relationship conflict
- Venue
- Voiceprints
- Voluntariness of a confession
- Voluntariness hearing: mishandling of
- When does the right counsel inure
- Youth of defendant as affecting knowledgeable plea

CHAPTER 7

7. Recommended Legal Books

INTRODUCTION

As this is the 2025 Prisoner Edition, I wanted to add these last two chapters specifically for all of those who are incarcerated.

Very few living in society think of the cause and effect that today's technology has on America's incarcerated population. And, really, why would you?

As technology continues to rapidly advance in the world and make accessing data, media, and information more and more convenient, today virtually anything you could possibly want to know can effortlessly be found on your phone or tablet. Printed publications as a direct result consequently are becoming more and more obsolete. Many printed publications are converting their magazines, newsletters, and books over to the Internet and discontinuing their printed products altogether. That might not mean much to you. Maybe you even prefer reading them on your tablet instead of getting them in the store or by mail. And as true as that is for many living in society, the real truth is that unfortunately, these technological advancements haven't yet reached the incarcerated population in most states, including my state, Pennsylvania.

For many of us who are incarcerated, even though tablets and other technologies are slowly being integrated into prisons, printed publications such as paperback books, magazines, newspapers, and newsletters are our primary source for information and entertainment. Therefore, I compiled these two lists of legal related publications for all of you that are incarcerated and don't have the luxury of having access to the Internet.

Note: Many of the listed books I've read, and I'm currently subscribed to many of the newsletters and magazines that I've included.

Punishment Without Trial: Why Plea Bargaining is a Bad Deal
Carissa Byrne Hessick

Plea Bargaining has been undermined at every turn and across the socioeconomic and racial divides. The consequences are dire. It has turned our legal system into a ruthlessly efficient mass incarceration machine. Hessick illustrates how plea bargaining has damaged our criminal justice system and sets out what we can do to fix it. Order online or from Edward R. Hamilton Bookseller Company, P.O. Box 15, Falls Village, CT, 06031-0015. 280 pages. $5.95

NOLO – Legal Research: How to Find and Understand the Law
Cara O'Neil

Showing you how to find statutes, cases, background information, and answers to specific legal questions online. Even more important, you'll be guided to the most reliable and user-friendly sites so you won't drown in an information flood. Order online or at Edward R. Hamilton Bookseller Company, P.O. Box 15, Falls Village, CT, 06031-0015. 356 pages. $37.95

NOLO – The Criminal Law Handbook: Know Your Rights, Survive the System, 17th Edition
Paul Bergman demystifies the complex rules and procedures of criminal law. It explains how the system works, why police, lawyers, and judges do what they do, and what suspects, defendants, and prisoners can expect. It also provides critical information on working with a lawyer. Order online or from Edward R. Hamilton Bookseller Company, P.O. Box 15, Falls Village, CT, 06031-0015. 642 pages. $29.95

Black's Law Dictionary
Bryan Garner

"One of the best overall criminal law dictionaries available. It's a must-have for any jailhouse lawyer or individual going through the criminal court system." - Sam

Order online or from Books n Things Warehouse, Inc., P.O. Box 7330, Shrewsbury, NJ, 07702. $44.95

NOLO – Represent Yourself in Court
Mike Twohy, Paul Bergman, Lisa Guerin, Sara J. Berman

Sometimes it makes sense to handle a court case without an attorney. Learn about acting as your own lawyer in Nolo's easy-to-use, plain-English guide, *Represent Yourself in Court*. This book breaks down the trial process into easy-to-understand steps so that you can act as your own lawyer safely and efficiently. Find out what to say, how to say it -- even where to stand when you address the judge and jury. Order online or from Books N' Things Warehouse, Inc., P.O. Box 7330, Shrewsbury, NJ, 07702. $39.99

Meister Manual for Prisoners' Lawsuits
David Meister

The Second Edition of "Battling the Administration: An inmate's guide to successful lawsuits" was renamed, revised, and updated in 2021 with new case law and current legal theory written from the prisoner's perspective. This book offers guidance on tips for investigating and building a case, detailed overview of the legal system, and more. Order online or from Edward R. Hamilton Bookseller Company, P.O. Box 15, Falls Village, CT, 06031. 711 pages. $29.95

The Best Resource Directory for Prisoners

Mike Enemigo

"A must-have reference book for any inmate!" – Sam

Contains over 1,400 up-to-date prisoner resources! Includes addresses for legal help, pen-pal companies, non-nude photo sellers, prisoner advocates, prisoner assistance, correspondence education, free books and other publications, money-making opportunities, resources for prison poets, writers, artists, and more! Order online or directly from The Cell Block, P.O. Box 1025, Rancho Cordova, CA, 95741. 296 pages. $17.95

Nolo – Criminal Law: A Desk Reference, 5ᵗʰ Edition

Paul Bergman

Covers the basics to the complex in alphabetical order. Whether it's "alibi: or "writ of habeas corpus," the reference makes it easy to find and understand what you're looking for. Order online or from Edward R. Hamilton Bookseller Company, P.O. Box 15, Falls Village, CT, 06031-0015. 446 pages. $32.95

Arrest-Proof Yourself, Second Edition

D. C. Carson & W. Denham

An ex-cop reveals how easy it is for anyone to get arrested, how even a single arrest could ruin your life, and what to do if approached by the police. It tells you everything you need to know about how cops operate, the little things that can get you in trouble, and much more. Order online or from Edward R. Hamilton Bookseller Company, P.O. Box 15, Falls Village, CT, 06031-0015. 376 pages. $14.95

Barron's Dictionary of Legal Terms: Definitions and Explanations for Non-Lawyers, 5ᵗʰ Edition

Steven H. Gifis

This cuts through the complexities of legal jargon and gives you definitions and explanations that you can understand. Here's a handy guide to "legalese" your consumers, business proprietors, legal beneficiaries, investors, property owners, litigants, and all others who have dealings with the law. Order online or from Edward R. Hamilton Bookseller Company, P.O. Box 15, Falls Village, CT, 06031-0015 640pages. $14.95

How to Think Like a Lawyer – And why: A Common Sense Guide to Everyday Dilemmas

Kim Wehle

This book has the answers to help you cut through the confusion and gain an advantage in your everyday life. Wehle identifies the details you need to pay attention to, the questions you should ask, the responses you should anticipate, and the pitfalls you can avoid. Order online or from Edward R. Hamilton Bookseller Company, Box 15, Falls Village, CT, 06031-0015. 167 pages $12.95

From Prison Grievances to Court: How to File and Win

Sophia J. Quill

You have a problem? Someone violate your rights? Can't write your loved ones in another prison? Peeved about your medical care? Trust fund issue? Missing jail time credits? If you have answered yes to any of these questions, this book is for you! Everything you want to know about filing and winning administrative remedies is included. Learn about BP-9s, the Freedom of Information Act, using the online prison law library, and how to exhaust your remedies in preparation for court are all covered in this book. Order online or from Freebird Publishers, 221 Pearl Street, Ste. 541, North Dighton, MA, 02764. 120 pages. $28.99, shipping included.

The PRO SE Guide to Legal Research & Writing

Raymond E. Lumsden

This easy-to-follow and understand guide provides you with the tools necessary to obtain relief in your legal issues. Clear, concise, and direct legal writing is essential for inmates, especially where the "deck is already stacked against you." Prison "writ-writers" tend to use opaque, jargon-filled writing, which only serves to further alienate those reading it. In this manner, relief is hard-pressed to obtain, if at all. If you want to win relief from your writing, this is the book for you. Order online or from Freebird Publishers, 221 Pearl Street, Ste. 541, North Dighton, MA, 02764. 95 pages. $24.99, shipping included.

Ineffective Assistance of Counsel: Overcoming the Inevitable

Kelly Patrick Riggs

This book is endorsed by the former Judge who wrote its foreword, and its material is used by thousands of legal professionals nationwide. It is also the first comprehensive lawman's guide written to explain the duty of counsel from initial appearances all the way through to direct appeal, and it is explained in plain English. With this book, the reader will be armed with the wisdom of hundreds of years of legal development. It contains the rules that the federal courts are supposed to follow in criminal cases and provides the laws and roles that govern the post-conviction procedures. Order online or from Freebird Publishers, 221 Pearl Street, Ste. 541, North Dighton, MA, 02764. 360+ pages. $36.99, shipping included.

The PRO SE Section 1983 Manual

Raymond E. Lumsden

This book is an invaluable and indispensable resource for the pro se inmate seeking to protect their constitutional rights in prison and obtaining reform. Written by an inmate for inmates, the Pro Se Section 1983 Manual is an authoritative, organized, and easy-to-understand manual designed to bring results and relief. Every inmate wishing to protect their civil rights should have a copy. Order online or from Freebird Publishers, 221 Pearl Street, Ste. 541, North Dighton, MA, 02764. 266 pages. $31.99, shipping included.

The Habeas Corpus Manual

Raymond E. Lumsden

This book is written specifically for the pro se inmate. Within the manual lay the necessary information, process, and instructions necessary to obtaining relief in your state from habeas corpus. From the initial investigation through the filing of your writ of habeas corpus, you are provided effective forms, motions, and detailed instructions specific to state-level habeas corpus. Armed with this book, relief is only a few pages away if done properly and effectively. Any pro se inmate serious about post-conviction relief should order a copy. Even if you're not incarcerated and are looking to overturn a conviction, sentence, etcetera, this book is for you. Order online or from Freebird Publishers, 221 Pearl Street, Ste. 541, North Dighton, MA, 02764. 273 pages. $31.99, shipping included.

The 7 Book Series: Post-Conviction Relief by Kelly Patrick Riggs

Book One: Post-Conviction Relief: Secrets Exposed

STOP: If you like prison, don't read this book! This book is full of information about how to get out of prison early. Cover-to-cover filled motions and secrets used by real habeas corpus practitioners getting real results. This book gives you what the courts don't want you to have, an understanding of the reason you're in prison. You'll learn the proper habeas corpus practice that courts follow rather than the fairy tale that's taught in school. Learn in plain English how to win in a Section 2255 proceeding. Includes real filings from real cases that have prevailed. Order online or from Freebird Publishers, 221 Pearl Street, Ste. 541, North Dighton, MA, 02764. 190+pages. $28.99

Book Two: Post-Conviction Relief: The Appeal

No Fairy Tales, just appeals

The appeals process taught to lawyers in layman's terms. Step-by-step, rule-by-rule, learn the appeal process.

- Notice of appeal
- Designation of the record
- Certificate of appealability
- Operational habits of the court clerks
- Briefs
- Rules
- Applicable laws, and much more.

Everything the pro se inmate needs to know about winning on appeal. Order online or from Freebird Publishers, 221 Pearl Street, Ste. 541, North Dighton, MA, 02764. 180+ pages. $28.99, shipping included.

Book Three: Post-Conviction Relief: Advancing Your Claim

This third book in the series is written to correct the most basic problem in your case, the way you think so many prisoners fail to obtain post-conviction relief, because they attempt to sound like a lawyer. That's a mistake. That's because the post-conviction relief process is designed to allow prisoners to express themselves plainly without being required to know laws and rules. This book is my effort to set a standard by which a layman can measure their ability to express themselves to a court effectively. This book will teach you how to present motions and petitions that are more pleasing to judges who, in most cases, want you to have what you deserve under the law. It will teach you how to refine your pleadings by understanding the importance of critical word usage and syllogistic reasoning. You will learn the importance of presenting a clear set of facts as opposed to a theory in law they already know. Order online or from Freebird Publishers, 221 Pearl Street, Ste. 541, North Dighton, MA, 02764. 218 pages. $28.99, including shipping.

Book Four: Post-Conviction Relief: Winning Claims

Seeking early release? Get examples of winning cases that have raised claims in every step of the criminal process. A homerun starts with a strong swing at a good pitch. In the post-conviction relief process, a homerun requires a constitutional error and your second claim. This book is provided to give beginners and new practitioners a head start. Included are hundreds of claims and cases of those who have won. Order online or from Freebird Publishers, 221 Pearl Street, Ste. 541, North Dighton, MA, 02764. 226 pages. $28.99 including shipping.

Book Five: Post-Conviction Relief: C.O.A. In the Supreme Court

Knowing is half the battle. Know the facts and improve your chances of being granted review in The Supreme Court of the United States. This addition to the Post-Conviction Relief Series is about preparation, and the first step to all successes is preparation. This book provides you with a head start by letting you know what the Supreme Court expects from you before the countdown begins. This book puts everything you need at your fingertips. It's a must-have for any jailhouse lawyer or pro se litigant. Order online or from Freebird Publishers, 221 Pearl Street, Ste. 541, North Dighton, MA, 02764. 180+ pages. $28.99 includes shipping.

Book Six: Post-Conviction Relief: Second Last Chance

At sentencing, defendants are informed of their right to appeal. After appeal, lawyers tell their clients about their right to file for post-conviction relief under 28 U.S.C. 2255, but not without laughter in their voice. What they don't tell their clients is that a 2255 motion cannot be based on actual innocence or over-sentencing. This book fills that gap. It explains how to take action for both actual innocence and over-sentencing along with explaining which legal mechanism to use. It breaks the fairytale about 2255's one-year statute of limitations. It explains how to determine which federal prisoners are among the thousands who are actually innocent of being over-sentenced. Order online or from Freebird Publishers, 221 Pearl Street, Ste. 541, North Dighton, MA, 02764. 180+ pages. $28.99 includes shipping.

Book Seven: Post-Conviction Relief: "The Advocate"

The final book in the Post-Conviction Relief Series by Kelly Patrick Riggs.
It's finally time to advance to a new station in life. You have read the first six books. I have written on the subject of post-conviction relief; thus, the training process is over. This is a lot like studying for a new job, and the time has come for you to enter the work force. To continue, you need the tools of your trade. This book contains many motions with explanations I have synthesized over the years to gain relief on behalf of many prisoners. Inside these covers, you'll   find all the tools you will need for your own practice as a prison paralegal. These are the nuts and boils for post-conviction relief in both state and federal proceedings. Order online or from Freebird Publishers, Freebird Publishers, 221 Pearl Street, Ste. 541, North Dighton, MA, 02764. 230+ pages. $28.99 including shipping.

Prison Legal Guide

Mike Enemigo

Mike Enemigo is one of the best incarcerated authors in the game! All his non-fiction books for prisoners are must-haves, but his Prison Legal Guide is probably the best. U. S. law is complex, complicated, and always growing and changing, and many prisoners spend days on end digging through its intricacies. Pile on top of the legal code the rules and regulations of a correctional facility, and you can see how well the deck is being stacked against you. Information is the key to your survival when you have run afoul of the system (or it is running afoul of you). Whether you are an accomplished jailhouse lawyer helping newbies learn the ropes, an old-head fighting bare-knuckled for your rights in the courts, or an inmate just looking to beat the latest writeup, this book has something for you!

With this information in hand, you are well equipped to beat the charge or fight back against the persecution. Learn about litigation, First Amendment status, due process in prison, cruel and unusual punishment, medical care, post-conviction, and much more. There are many of us out here on your side. Never give up the fight. Order online or from either Freebird Publishers, 221 Pearl Street, Ste. 541, North Dighton, MA, 02764, or The Cell Block, P.O. Box 1025, Rancho Cordova, CA, 95741. 201+pages. $33.99 includes shipping.

Prisoner's Self-Help Litigation Manual, 4th Edition
Dan Manville
The premiere, must-have "bible" of prison litigation for current and aspiring jailhouse lawyers. If you plan to litigate a prison or jail civil lawsuit, this is the book you need. The author, Dan Manville, is a former prisoner who got out and became a lawyer and teaches college students. Order online or from Prison Legal News, P. O. Box 1151, Lake Worth, FL, 33460. 1500 pages. $39.95

Jailhouse Lawyers: Prisoners Defending Prisoners v. The USA
Mumia Abu-Jamal
In "Jailhouse Lawyers," Prison Legal News columnist, award-winning journalist and former death-row prisoner Mumia Abu-Jamal presents the stories and reflections of fellow prisoners-turned-advocates who have learned to use the court system to represent other prisoners, and in some cases, have won their freedom. A must-read for jailhouse lawyers! Order online or from Prison Legal News, P. O. Box 1151, Lake Worth, FL, 33460. 280 pages. $16.95

The Jailhouse Lawyer's Handbook
Written by The Center for Constitutional Rights staff.
This book explains how a prisoner in a state correctional facility can file a lawsuit in federal court to fight against mistreatment and bad conditions. The handbook discusses only one kind of legal problem which prisoners face – the problem of prison conditions and the way prisoners are treated by prison staff.
5th Edition has transgender and immigrant rights information. Order online at www.jailhouselaw.org or by writing to Jailhouse Lawyers Handbook, c/o The Center for Constitutional Rights, 666 Broadway, 7th Floor, New York, NY, 10012.

Jailhouse Lawyer's Manual, 10th Edition
It is a comprehensive guide to legal rights and procedures written for the use of incarcerated individuals. Prisoners are often indigent and therefore lack access to legal counsel while incarcerated. The JLM informs prisoners of their legal rights, shows them how to secure these rights through the

judicial process, and guides them through the complex array of procedures and legal vocabulary which makes up this system. With the JLM, prisoners can learn to use effectively the resources available in the prison law libraries.

The Jailhouse Lawyer's Manual publishes three books, all designed for prisoners to understand their rights and help them navigate the justice system.

The Jailhouse Lawyer's Manual, 10th Edition, is the main volume. It's a guide that has more than 1,000 pages of valuable information to help you learn about: Researching the law; Appealing Your Conviction or Sentence; Receiving Medical Care, Protecting Your Civil Liberties, and much more. 1288 pages.

$30.00 (for prisoners only) or $100 (for non-prisoners or institutions).

The Immigration Supplement is a supplement to the main JLM volume and contains information about immigration law and the rights of non-citizens. 116 pages. $5.00 (for prisoners only)

The Texas Supplement is a supplement to the main JLM volume and contains specific information for Texas State prisoners. 408 pages. $20 (for prisoners only)

Order online at www.law.columbia.edu/hrlr/jlm/order or by writing them at: Columbia Human Rights Law Review, Jailhouse Lawyer's Manual, 435 West 116th Street, New York, NY, 10027.

Battling The Administration

David Meister

"Great book to have on hand for any inmate." – Sam

This book is an inmate's guide to a successful lawsuit, written from a prisoner's perspective. This book is excellent for both the first-time litigant and the professional jailhouse lawyer when it comes to navigating the complex world of prisoners' rights. Order online or from Wynword Press, P. O. Box 557, Bonners Ferry, ID, 83805. 555 pages. $34.95.

The Criminal Law Handbook: Know Your Rights, Survive the System

Paul Bergman and Sara J. Berman-Barrett

This book breaks down the civil trial process in easy-to-understand steps so you can effectively represent yourself in court. The authors explain what to say in court, how to say it, etcetera. Order online or from Prison Legal News, P. O. Box 1151, Lake Worth, FL, 33460. 528 pages. $39.99

Criminal Law in a Nutshell, 5th Edition

Arnold Loewy

Provides an overview of criminal law, including punishment, specific crimes, defenses, and burden of proof. Order online or from Prison Legal News, P. O. Box 1151, Lake Worth, FL, 33460. 387 pages. $43.95

The Habeas Citebook: Ineffective Assistance of Counsel

Brandon Sample and Alissa Hull

This is Prison Legal News' second published book which exclusively covers ineffective assistance of counsel-related issues in federal habeas petitions. Great resource for habeas litigation with hundreds of case citations. Order online or directly from Prison Legal News, P. O. Box 1151, Lake Worth, FL, 33460. 200 pages. $49.95

Marijuana Law

Examines how to reduce the possibility of arrest and prosecution for people accused of the use, sale, or possession of marijuana. This book includes information on legal defenses, search and seizures, surveillance, asset forfeiture, and drug testing. Order online or from Prison Legal News, P. O. Box 1151, Lake Worth, FL, 33460. 271 pages. $17.95

The Prisoner's Guide to Survival

L. Powell Belanger

This is a comprehensive legal assistance manual for post-conviction relief and prisoners' civil rights. Order online or from PSI Publishing, 413-B 19th Street, Ste. 168, Lynden, WA, 98264. 750 pages. $49.95 plus $5.00 S/H

Great Tips for Prisoners to Get a Fast Parole

If you're incarcerated and behind bars, your most compelling dream and desire is to get out and be free once again. This guide is written by a former prisoner who successfully applied these legal principles to his own situation and achieved an early parole due to his knowledge and persistence. Discover the exact way he did it! Send $15.99 (FREE shipping) to Strategic Parole Solutions, P.O. Box 8363, Fort Worth, TX, 76124.

Recommended Legal Newsletters and Magazines for Prisoners

Outlook on Justice

2161 Massachusetts Avenue
Cambridge, MA 02140
Details: The AFCS publishes a 24-page quarterly magazine "Outlook on Justice." It's only $2.00 for a year. (4 issues)

The Angolite

Louisiana State Penitentiary
Angola, LA 70712
Details: The Angolite newsletter is an award-winning inmate-published and edited publication. It's $20.00 for a year. (6 issues)

The Fire Inside

1540 Market Street, Ste. 490

San Francisco, CA 94102

Details: The California Coalition for Women Prisoners runs an action center and publishes a quarterly newsletter FREE to women.

Coalition for Prisoners' Rights

P.O. Box 1911

Santa Fe, NM 87504

(Phone) 505-982-9520

Details: The Prisoners' Rights-Prison Project of Santa Fe. A monthly newsletter FREE to all currently and formally incarcerated individuals and their families. However, stamps and donations are needed.

Criminal Legal News

P. O. Box 1151

Lake Worth, FL 33460

Website: www.criminallegalnews.org

Details: The people who bring you Prison Legal News proudly announce the introduction of its companion publication, Criminal Legal News. The same timely, relevant, and practical legal news as PLN, but CLN provides legal news you can use about the criminal justice system prior to confinement and post-conviction relief. Criminal Legal News is a 40-page monthly newsletter published by the Human Rights Defense Center, a (c) (3) nonprofit human rights organization that zealously advocates, educates, and litigates on issues pertaining to prisoners' and individual's rights. $48 a year (for prisoners) or $5.00 for a single or back issue.

California Lifer Newsletter

P. O. Box 277

Rancho Cordova, CA 95741

(Phone) 916-402-3750

Website: www.lifesupportalliance.org

Details: CLN is a newsletter that's published six times a year. It includes reviews of the latest published and unpublished state and federal cases concerning parole issues, along with many more topics of interest to prisoners. Special discounted rate for prisoners. $30 for a year (6 issues) or 60 first-class Forever stamps.

California Prison Focus

1904 Franklin Street, Ste. 507
Oakland, CA 94612
(Phone) 510-836-7222
Website: www.prisons.org
Details: "Our newsletter magazine is primarily by prisoners and for prisoners, their families and friends. The current and past issues are available FREE for download. You can also receive a paper copy. We request a donation of $20 or more for 4 issues to help cover editing, printing, and mailing costs."

The Fortune Society

29-76 Norther Blvd.
Long Island City, NY 11101-2822
Details: Helps ex-prisoners break the cycle of crime and incarceration and educates the public about prison and the cause and effect of crime. FREE newsletter for prisoners.

Georgetown ARCP

600 New Jersey Ave NW
Washington, DC 20001
Details: The Georgetown Law Journal Annual Review of Criminal Procedures is a topic-by-topic summary of criminal procedures in the United States Supreme Court and each of the 12 Federal Circuit Courts of Appeal. The publication costs $15

Graterfriends

Pennsylvania Prison Society
245 N. Broad St., Ste. 300
Philadelphia, PA 19107
Website: www.prisonsociety.org
Details: This is a great newsletter relating to prisons and prisoners' issues. Subscriptions are only $3.00 (for prisoners)

Fair Chance News

1137 E. Redondo Blvd
Inglewood, CA 90302
Details: Fair Chance Project represents a movement led by liberated lifers, their families, and concerned community members advocating for just sentencing laws and fair parole practices. Sen $5 or $5 worth of stamps for your prisoner membership which includes a newsletter titled Fair Chance News.

FAMMgram
Families Against Mandatory Minimum
1100 H Street NW, Ste. 1000
Washington, DC 20005
Website: www.famm.org
Details: Quarterly newsletter for $10 per year (for prisoners)

MS Magazine
ATTN: MS In Prison Program
1600 Wilson Blvd., Ste. 801
Arlington, VA 22209
MS is a feminist publication covering current events, politics, and culture. Women in prison can get a FREE membership by writing the above address.

The New Abolitionist
P. O. Box 151-F
Fennimore, WI 53809
Details: Newsletter of Prisoners Action Coalition. Good contact for prison issues in Wisconsin, has experience dealing with super max issues.

Off Our Backs Magazine
2337-B 18th Street NW
Washington, DC 20009
Details: A radical feminist news journal FREE to women in prison

Outlook on Justice
Publication of Criminal Justice Program of the AFSC
2161 Massachusetts Avenue
Cambridge, MA 02140
(Phone) 617-661-6130, ext. 120
Details: A newsletter of the American Friends Services Committee. It's $2.00 for a year (for prisoners). 4 magazines /newsletter.

Prison Legal News
P. O. Box 11151
Lake Worth, FL 33460
Website: www.prisonlegalnews.org
Details: PLN reports on legal cases and news stories related to prisoner rights and prison conditions of confinement. PLN welcomes all news clippings, legal summaries, and leads on people to contact related to those issues. Article submissions should be sent to The Editor at

the above address. PLN is a monthly publication, and a one-year subscription is $30 for prisoners, $35 for individuals, and $90 for lawyers and institutions.

San Francisco Bay View

Willie Ratcliff, Publisher
4917 Third Street
San Francisco, CA 94124-2309
Website: www.sfbayview.com
Details: Bay View is an independent newspaper of liberation journalism. Subscribe for $24 per year, $12 for six months, or $2.00 per month. Make checks payable to Bay View. You may also pay in postage stamps. To our readers behind enemy lines: If you have no funds or stamps, your annual subscription request can be paid from the Prisoners Subscription Fund when donations are sufficient. Pen Pal ads are FREE to prisoners!

San Quentin News

1 Main Street
San Quentin, CA 94964
Details: San Quentin News is a 16-page monthly newsletter written, edited, and produced by prisoners incarcerated at San Quentin State Prison. The SQ News encourages prisoners, staff, and others outside the institution to submit articles, poems, artwork, and letters to the editor for possible inclusion. To receive a mailed copy of the SQ News, send $1.32 in postage. This process should be repeated every month for each new edition.

Southland Prison News

955 Massachusetts Avenue, PMB 339
Cambridge, MA 02139
Details: This is a newsletter that covers prisoner news in the East and Southern states. It's $15 per year.

State v. US Magazine

P. O. Box 29291
Baltimore, MD 21213
Website: www.statevsusmag.com
Details: State v. US is an online and print publication that spotlights high-profile cases, corruption in prisons, police departments, and other branches of the government, wrongful convictions, true stories of men and women in prison, and success stories of formally incarcerated individuals. If you have a story to tell, email them, or write to the address above. They also sell advertising space if you have a product to promote. State v. US was nominated for the 2018 and 2019 Titan Award for magazine of the year. The print magazine is high-quality,

full color, and each issue is $10.99, or you can subscribe to the next 4 issues for $35.00. It comes out quarterly.

The Prison Mirror

c/o Pat Pawlak
970 Pickett Street North
Bayport, MN 55003-1490
(Phone) 631-779-2700
The Prison Mirror is published monthly by and for the men of the Minnesota Stillwater Correctional Facility. Annual subscriptions are $12. The Prison Mirror was founded in 1887 and is the oldest continuously published prison newspaper in the United States.

Abolitionist Newsletter

P. O. Box 22780
Oakland, CA 94609
(Phone) 510-444-0484
Website: www.criticalresistance.org
Details: Critical Resistance bilingual paper is called The Abolitionist, written mainly by prisoners, former prisoners, and community advocates. This paper is a medium for prisoners and community members to grapple with the present-day reality of the prison industrial complex, to understand its relationship to what's happening in our various communities, and to figure out what it will take for us to realize a world without cages. $15 for a year (3 issues).

Prison Life Magazine

P. O. Box 4845
Frankfort, KY 40604
(Phone) 502-353-4138
Website: www.prisonlifemagazine.com
Details: Published by Good Acres Sanctuary with the Commonwealth of Kentucky content restrictions. This magazine is a quarterly publication for America's incarcerated, parolees, ex-felons, and their families. $25 for a year (4 issues). Digital online subscription, $6.00.

Returning Citizens Magazine

15000 Potomac Town Place, Ste. 813
Woodbridge, VA 22191
(Phone) 877-871-4172
Website: www.returningcitizensmag.com
Details: This newer magazine provides information on topics like expungement, second-chance housing and jobs, and other needed re-entry programs. Subscriptions are available in

print and digitally. $29.99 for a year (4 issues). Can be ordered online or by mail. Checks accepted by mail payable to Scalable Consulting, LLC.

Vanguard Incarcerated Press

Davis Vanguard
P. O. Box 4715
Davis, CA 95617
Website: www.davaisvanguard.org
Details: A FREE newsletter for prisoners, VIP features hard-hitting and uncensored news from incarcerated people enabling prisoners to have a voice. VIP consists of two 2-sided color letter-size pages. Sent out 24 times per year.

ABOUT THE AUTHOR

About The Author

Sam is the founder of the publishing company, The Prisoner Press, and author of the popular book series "The Shit Prisoners Need to Know." Currently an inmate at a state correctional facility in Frackville, Pennsylvania, Sam is halfway through serving a six-year prison term.

Can one individual, especially an incarcerated one, do any good or make a difference? In Sam's own words: "Truthfully, I don't know, but as it's evident with my books, I'm determined to try and do everything I possibly can to improve the future successes of ex-offenders and the lives of prisoners, and provide them all with what they require more than anything, the thing that no one else wants them to have, and that's the Game Plan, tools, and knowledge necessary to build successful and prosperous new lives for themselves in the most unlikely of places and against all odds."

Sam has spent nearly an entire decade behind bars since his first prison stint in 2012 at the age of only 20, and has spent even longer as a drug addict living the criminal lifestyle in Philadelphia. Today, Sam has risen above that and is now well regarded as an expert on subjects pertaining to physical, mental, and emotional afflictions that are associated with incarceration, long term institutionalization, addiction, as well as the criminal mind.

In addition to managing his publishing company and writing books from his prison cell, Sam keeps himself active throughout his institution by providing legal assistance to those who need it, running workshops for aspiring and incarcerated entrepreneurs and authors, and teaching his own financial education class where he provides inmates the important fundamentals of credit, banking, budgeting, and investing. Sam is a beacon of hope to all prisoners and ex-offenders who aspire to become successful, and furthermore is proof that with the right knowledge, mindset, and determination, you can achieve wealth and success even in the least likely of places under the worst possible circumstances. Upon his release from prison in 2028, Sam has big plans for his future, including further expanding the reach of his educational platform and, through his company, creating opportunities for incarcerated entrepreneurs and authors to become successful, not only in prison, but out in the world as well. Sam has moved away from his old life and has achieved incredible success for himself since being incarcerated. As he is single and currently without children, he looks forward to getting out on parole for the very last time. He would like to find the right woman to start a family with, settle down, and enjoy his new life. This is something he never thought could be possible because of the dangerous and unpredictable fast criminal lifestyle he had lived for most of his life.

ABOUT THE SERIES

About The Series

When I first came up with the idea of creating a series of books that would help prisoners and ex-offenders with a variety of useful and important things that they need to know both while in prison and once they're back out on the streets, it was just another project to keep me busy. I honestly never expected it to ever go any further than the inside of one of my record center boxes under the bunk where all my artwork, poems, and other projects end up once I'm done with them. As an inmate myself who's disconnected and cut off from the outside world with only limited communication to friends and loved ones, I understand that there is so much information and resources available that could significantly help to improve prisoners' lives while they're doing their time in prison that they simply have no way of knowing even exists, and those who do know won't ever tell "us" about it.

That's how I came up with the name THE SHIT PRISONERS NEED TO KNOW, a true-enough title that every one of "us," whether you're a prisoner or an ex-offender, can relate to. I had naturally assumed that there were hundreds of similar kinds of helpful resource books available for prisoners. My first step was to size up the competition. No reason to even start the project if there were already an abundance of books out there just like mine on the off-chance that I did end up wanting to publish it, so I reached out to my people for help looking up all the current prisoner help and ex-offender re-entry books available online. Being in prison, we are restricted from using the Internet for any reason, even though many of us actually have legitimate needs for accessing the Internet, such as researching legal, business, and other just as important information that we need, like looking for housing, employment, and applying for benefits before getting released.

I was really shocked at just how few there were of up-to-date books for prisoners. Most of them were old and outdated, written years before the pandemic. Although I knew that between Amazon and Google, if a book exists, they would definitely be able to find it. Still, I couldn't believe that there weren't more current prisoner resource books, especially regarding finances, credit and money, re-entry, housing, and employment, so I signed up for the library to do my own search. I figured that if anyplace would have the most up-to-date collection of books for prisoners, it would be a prison library. But after searching through the entire book catalog on the library computer and coming up with nothing but even more out-of-date books, some even written as far back as the '80s and '90s, I realized right then and there that my idea of creating a series of how-to guides and resource directories for prisoners and ex-offenders was no longer just going to be another project that ends up in a box.

I knew that there was a real need for all the books I planned to write in the series. So far, there are a total of four books planned for the series, with the first book published, the second going on sale in the summer of 2025, and the third in the works right now. It was one of those rare "if you build it, they will come" kind of moment for me. I knew that I needed to create this series and write books that as a prisoner I would want to read and that would help benefit me -- books with relevant articles, how-to guides, and up-to-date information and resources about real things that would benefit and help prisoners that otherwise most wouldn't be able to find on their own.

The most important thing about prisoners is that most of them don't stay prisoners forever, and eventually they are released and turn into parolees and ex-offenders, where I would strongly argue the real struggle begins once they are back out on the streets. Because of that, with the success of my original version of this directory, I wanted to create a special Jailhouse Lawyer Edition where I also include prisoner-specific and re-entry resources that both incarcerated individuals and ex-offenders back out in the community can benefit greatly from.

Every book in the series is important in its own way, but my first book, THE NATIONAL PRO BONO ATTORNEY DIRECTORY, is all around the most important book for everyone, not just felons or ex-offenders who are struggling to find legal aid to get their life where they want it to be. What puts every book I write on a level of its own, way above the rest, isn't just because there aren't many books out there right now that can actually compete or that mine are simply much better than the few current books that are out there. It's because you know everything within my books can be trusted to be accurate, and everything that I speak on I've either been through or have done myself probably on more than just one occasion.

My books, even this very directory, aren't just general how-to-do this to get this kind of

book or just a bunch of facts, information and resources, although, yeah, most of them do have a lot of that stuff inside. They also have me and, more importantly, my own personal knowledge, experience, including both my successes and failures, insight, stories, and advice on all the things in life that I know so much about. Who knew that being a "bad guy" living the criminal fast lifestyle would actually one day benefit not only me but so many others who are just like me in a legitimate way, that all my insider knowledge and over a decade's worth of real like experience dealing with every aspect of the American Criminal Justice System, Department of Corrections and parole would be put to good use to help prisoners, parolees, ex-offenders and addicts better themselves and learn how to thrive inside prison and become successful once they are released and back out on the street.

When I was researching other books similar to the one I wanted to write for the series, besides discovering that there weren't nearly enough of them, I was just as surprised to discover that every ex-offender re-entry and prison help book I found was written by just about every other type of person except for the one type who actually should write them, which is those who have actually been in the shoes of the very people that they are writing books for, prisoners, parolees, and ex-offenders. I couldn't believe out of all the books, not one single author was an ex-offender. I think it's a little fucked up how all these "normal" people who really don't know shit about what it's like being a prisoner or an ex-offender are profiting off people like you and me.

They write books explaining how to make it out in the world on parole and as an ex-offender when they themselves have likely never even been arrested, let alone experience what it's really like to return to society after having been locked away in prison for years. They can't truly relate or even understand the psychological shock and difficulty it is for an ex-offender to try and process the sudden change from waking up in prison to a few hours later being released and right back on the streets, all the while having to deal with the enormous challenges that come with trying to piece together an entirely new life.

Anyone can put together a book with a bunch of statistics, general re-entry information and national and state resources and call it a re-entry book. In fact, basically every one that I've read so far is exactly that: all basic facts without any real substance from actually people like me who have been there, done it, and have the scars, emotional baggage, and prison numbers to show for it. Put it this way: If my professional resume was anywhere near as extensive and accomplished as my criminal resume is, I'd pretty much be able to land a top position at any Fortune 500 company that I wanted, making billions of dollars a year. Unfortunately, my criminal experience doesn't transfer over to professional experience, but it does make me the most qualified to write about all my experiences in having gone through all of the various levels as a repeat "client" of the American Criminal Justice System, Incorporated, and its subsidiary company, The Department of Corrections.

I wrote this book, not because I wanted to cash out from writing about my own personal experiences as both a criminal and state inmate or to create a new, popular trending prisoner book series for profit. Contrary to what you might think, you don't get rich off writing these types of non-fiction books, especially when you're doing everything from your prison cell like I am. Unlike the rest of the authors, I've been about that life and know how hard it can be to do time, to make parole, to get out and have to start all over again with nothing, and I certainly understand all too well how challenging it can be to find good legal aid, especially if you can't afford to hire an attorney.

I wish that I had a book like this the first time I had been charged with a felony and had no other choice but to be represented by a public defender. Just maybe if I had, then I might have been able to find a pro bono attorney, and I never would've taken the plea deal that sent me to prison for my very first time. Since that pivotal moment in my life, I've been locked up in nine different county jails and seven state prisons. Admittedly, so far, every time that I've returned back into the community from prison, I've never actually succeeded in my re-entry journey. But yet, here I am writing an entire series of books on, among other things, helping you succeed at re-entry. I might have never been able to succeed myself, but I know what it takes. And besides, if you learn anything from my experience, it certainly will be what not to do when you get out. That's my real motivation behind writing this book and every other book in the series -- to help you become the best version of yourself by sharing my knowledge and insight and also by learning from all of my epic mistakes to not be like me but be better than me.

CONTACT
US

Contact Us

CONTACT THE PRISONER PRESS

THE PRISONER PRESS
P.O. BOX 6053
CLEARWATER, FL 33758

Find the newest releases, book details, information, and more at: theprisonerpress.com

CONTACT AUTHOR SAM FERRARO

Write him at:
SAM FERRARO QP4526
SMART COMMUNICATION/PADOC
P.O. BOX 33028
ST. PETERSBURG, FL 33733

Email him at: samf@theprisonerpress.com
Direct message him at: www.commectnetwork.com
Go to the website and set up an email account to connect directly with Sam. Click "Pennsylvania Department of Corrections." Search "Samuel Ferraro" or by his institution number "QP4526." Select "add inmate" and then fill out your email address and finish setting up your account. Once complete, you'll be able to send a direct message to Sam's tablet.

Thanks for Your Interest in
The Prisoner Press

We value our customers and would like to hear from you! We strive for the best, so reviews are an important tool in bringing you quality publications. We want to know our readers' opinions on whether you think it's good or not.

If you could take the time to review/rate any of the publications you've read from The Prisoner Press, we would appreciate it. If your loved ones use Amazon, have them post your review on the books you've read, and using Amazon's five-star rating system, post your rating. This will help us tremendously in providing future publications that are even more useful and informative to our readers and growing our business.

THE BEST FINANCIAL GUIDE FOR PRISONERS!

$19.99

THE
JAILHOUSE
FINANCIAL
PLAYBOOK

Game Changing Prisoner Money Making, Credit
Building, Debt Removing, Financial Secrets & Legal
Loopholes EXPOSED!

SAM FERRARO
FOREWORD BY D.T. HOLT

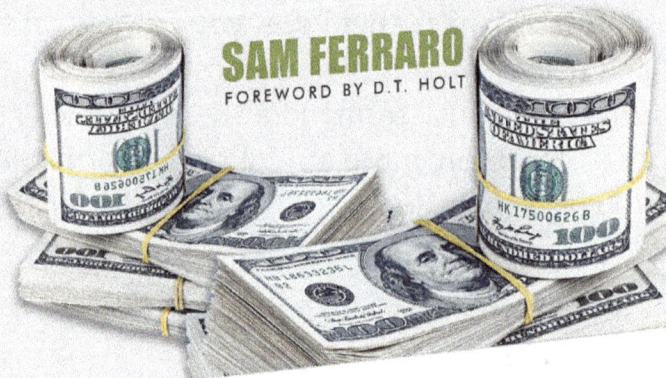

Considered to be the best financial guide for prisoners, the Jailhouse Financial Playbook is the second installment of Sam Ferraro's popular book series; The Shit Prisoners Need To Know. Sam is an incarcerated author whose work is based on the single principle of teaching prisoners and ex-offenders how to become successful through his own life experiences, hard learnt lessons, and the journey's he's had on both sides of the prison wall. In his newest financial guide, Sam exposes legal loopholes, shares secrets, and teaches you his proven game plan that he has used to successfully take back financial control of his life, and, ultimately, against insurmountable odds, achieve wealth and success all while incarcerated.

In this book you'll learn:

- Personal money management courses that teaches why you should care about your credit, how to easily improve your credit score hundreds of points for free, and use it responsibly.
- Step-by-step game plans teaching you everything you need to know to become financially independent and how to safeguard your money in prison.
- Exposes all the legal loopholes that they don't want you to know about in the Fair Credit Reporting Act (FCRA) to remove all of your debt in just 30 days.
- Breaks down all of your financial rights as a prisoner
- BONUS lesson for Pennsylvania state inmates on ACT 84, the law pertaining to it, facts that you need to know, and how you may be eligible to stop your institution from deducting 25% of all your money for court costs, fines, and restitution. Including Motion forms to stop ACT 84 and get reimbursed.
- Provides you with the insider knowledge to navigate around the strict DOC polices, cut through the red tape, and sidestep the obstacles that the prison may throw at you in your pursuit of becoming a successful jailhouse entrepreneur.
- Helps you navigate around the strict DOC polices, cut through the red tape, and side step the obstacles that the prison may throw at you in your pursuit of becoming a successful jailhouse entrepreneur.

The Jailhouse Financial Playbook isn't only educational for all those who are currently incarcerated, but for ex-offenders, and anyone else who's seeking financial success, but doesn't know where to begin. It provides you with the crucial information and resources that you need to start making the kind of intelligent, informed financial decisions that can change the trajectory of the rest of your life. Every inmate serious about the success of their future should have a copy of this book in their cell.

ON SALE NOW

TO GET YOUR COPY OF THE JAILHOUSE FINANCIAL PLAYBOOK, HAVE YOUR FAMILY OR FRIENDS GO ONLINE AND ORDER THE BOOK DIRECTLY FROM Order directly from www.theprisonerpress.com or anywhere books are sold.

ONLY $19.95 + FREE S/H) OR THROUGH EITHER AMAZON OR BARNES & NOBLE.

We do not accept any mailed-in book orders. Please do not send a book order or check to our company's P.O. Box. We will not process it. To order the book by mail, please write to Freebird Publishers or Edward R. Hamilton Bookseller. All other mail correspondence other than book orders can be sent to our company's P.O. Box.

**Order directly from www.theprisonerpress.com
or anywhere books are sold.**

For institutional mail in orders please send to either Freebird Publishers or Edward R. Hamilton bookseller.

www.ingramcontent.com/pod-product-compliance
Lightning Source LLC
Chambersburg PA
CBHW081810200326
41597CB00023B/4206